FANS FROM THE EAST

Claude Monet
La Japonaise 1876
Courtesy of the
Museum of
Fine Arts, Boston

FANS FROM THE EAST

Debrett's Peerage
in association with
The Fan Circle and
The Victoria & Albert Museum

© Debrett's Peerage Ltd 1978
Published by
Debrett's Peerage Ltd, 23 Mossop Street, London SW3
for the Birmingham City Museum and Art Gallery
and the Victoria & Albert Museum, London
in association with The Fan Circle.

Designed by Sinc and printed in England
by Raithby Lawrence and Co Ltd, Leicester and London

ISBN 0 905649 22 2 Hardback
ISBN 0 905649 21 4 Paperback

Contents

Foreword

'Fans from the East' commemorates the exhibition of the same name held at the Museum and Art Gallery, Birmingham, and the Victoria and Albert Museum, London, in 1978 and early 1979.

We are especially grateful to the Fan Circle and their patron, Lady Rosse, for organising the exhibition which this book complements. We would also like to thank Lady Rosse for lending so many splendid examples from the Messel Collection, a selection of which was last seen at the V&A in 1967.

We hope that the knowledge and scholarship that the book and exhibition encompass will increase the appreciation of the art of the oriental fan.

Roy Strong
Director, Victoria and Albert Museum

Dennis Farr
Director, Museum and Art Gallery, Birmingham

Introduction by the Countess of Rosse

Fans have been in existence since earliest civilised times. Europeans regarded them essentially as accessories of fashionable dress, increasingly so in the course of the eighteenth and nineteenth centuries. As such they were often objects of beauty and exquisite craftsmanship constructed with immense ingenuity out of a great variety of materials, the leaves decorated with vivid vignettes, classical or contemporary and the sticks carved with an intricate delicacy often in ivory, mother-of-pearl or tortoiseshell. They may not have attracted artists of the highest calibre but they are applied art at its most skilful and refined.

Fans from China and Japan have a greater meaning; they are not fashionable feminine accessories but symbols of significance in social and religious life which have inspired the greatest artists of their times. The early Eastern military fans often of heavy varied metals count not only as major status symbols for use by men of importance but could also be employed in the last resort as lethal weapons. In addition to the actual beauty and fascination of the seventeenth and eighteenth century oriental fan, they often tell an allegorical story. It is the endless variety of mood in these that grips the imagination. From the lonely figures in a gaming scene, from graceful ladies consorting together in a background of daily life, fabulous birds and frightening beasts, tender branches of trees or delicate flowers down to the brightly coloured crowds on the Mandarin fans, all tell their own sad or happy story of culture in a galaxy of exquisite craftsmanship.

I was fortunate to be brought up with a collection rich in fine examples from Europe and the Far East. It was formed by my father, Lt.-Col. L. C. R. Messel, who had a profound knowledge of Eastern arts and his explanations of the scenes on the fans made them memories of enduring delight to me. Our Fan Circle hopes that this book and the exhibition it commemorates will give something of the same pleasure to many and at the same time convey the traditions and beauty of the arts of the East.

We are grateful to all those who have worked so hard and with such profound knowledge to make this possible.

Fans from the East

Just over a hundred years ago, in 1870, the South Kensington Museums mounted the first international loan exhibition of fans under the patronage of Queen Victoria. It was an attempt to show them as works of aesthetic quality and craftsmanship, worthy of study by contemporary artists and *objets de vertu* in their own right, not just frivolous feminine accessories. This exhibition generated the enthusiasm which led Lady Charlotte Schreiber to form a fine collection, which was published in *Fans and Fan Leaves*, 1888, now in the Department of Prints and Drawings at the British Museum, and Leonard Messel to gather the fine Oriental and European fans and fan leaves which were displayed at the Victoria and Albert Museum in 1967. These private collections, which have mercifully remained intact together with the Victoria and Albert's own holdings, shared between the Department of Textiles and Dress, the Department of Prints and Drawings, the Far Eastern and Indian Sections, form the nucleus of the exhibition which has prompted this book.

After the heyday of late Victorian enthusiasm, fan collecting drifted into the generalised and romantic world of the Edwardian amateur of *bimbeloterie* and in the middle years of the present century went into an almost complete decline. In the very different economic and intellectual climate of today, the century and the cycle having turned full circle, a new generation are forming collections from the dispersed remnants of the old. Once again fans make regular and high priced appearances in the international sale rooms.

Five years ago the Fan Circle was formed to bring together the collector and his professional colleagues in museums. Small but enthusiastic, it organised an exhibition, 'The World of the Fan', at Preston Museum and Art Gallery in 1976 and has now embarked on the ambitious project, 'Fans from the East', an exhibition held at the Museum and Art Gallery, Birmingham, 1978–9, and at the Victoria and Albert Museum in early 1979.

Over the years it had become apparent that fans had attracted an interest more affectionate than analytical and it was hoped that a combination of orientalists working on sources relating to the origin of fans, museum curators, and collectors could begin the slow process of retrieving them from the backwater of dilettante chit-chat and nudge them towards the main stream of art and historical studies.

Only a small beginning has been made but it is already apparent that fans appear in so many guises, perform such a variety of functions and are so complex in manufacture that there is not one story here but a multitude. Fans are microcosms of the fine and the applied arts, reflecting with peculiar fidelity the nuances of a complex cultural interaction between East and West. Already we have had to jettison a few of the picturesque legends so lovingly retailed by the collectors of the past, but I hope that we have succeeded in replacing them with the romance of real life and the excitement of research without which there can be no real connoisseurship.

Madeleine Ginsburg
Chairman, Fan Circle
Assistant Keeper (Dress), Victoria and Albert Museum

Colour plates

Colour plates

Chapter 1

1 Folding fan, of 'hidden scene' type, ink and light colours on paper, bamboo sticks.
Chinese, late nineteenth century.
When opened in the normal manner from left to right, this fan depicts a woman and attendant in a garden.
By courtesy of Martin Willcocks.

2 Cabriolet fan, painted paper, enamelled gilt filigree sticks.
Chinese, for the Western market, early nineteenth century.
The depiction of Chinese and foreign ships was a popular subject amongst Chinese painters working for the Western market.
The Messel collection, by courtesy of the Countess of Rosse.

3 Screen fan, one of a pair, embroidered appliqués on gilt thread, tortoiseshell and bamboo frame.
Chinese, early nineteenth century.
By courtesy of the Victoria and Albert Museum.

4 Fan painting, ink and colour on paper.
Signed Pai-shih shan-weng. Ch'i Pai-shih (1863–1957).
Chinese, late nineteenth century or early twentieth century.
By courtesy of the Ashmolean Museum.

Chapter 2

5 *Hiogi* (court fan) of thirty-eight blades, decorated with a pine, crane and hairy-tailed tortoise (*minogame*), all symbolic of longevity, amid stylized clouds.
The antiquarian revival of the seventeenth century encouraged the use at court of the *hiogi*, which had been losing out in popularity to the more convenient paper folding fan. Although the design is traditional, the very large number of blades and the exaggerated length of the decorative silk threads (only partially visible here) point to a nineteenth century date.
By courtesy of the Victoria and Albert Museum.

6 Sakai Hoitsu (1761–1828).
A branch of maple. After a varied painting education Hoitsu found his true vocation in the Rimpa style, named after the famous decorative painter Ogata Korin (1658–1716), which uses for its effects, among other things, large flat areas of colour, especially gold and silver. Unsigned, with a seal *Hoitsu*.
From the collection of R. A. Harari, OBE.

7 Yamada Hogyoku (working circa 1820–1840).
Preparing for moon viewing. This print by an obscure artist known to us otherwise only through a small number of illustrated books exemplifies the deft placing and telling characterization which is a feature of much work of the Shijo school. The items shown, pampas grass, *sake* bottles and rice cakes, are traditionally associated with the moon viewing which takes place on the fifteenth day of the eighth month. Colour print from wood blocks.
Signed *Hogyoku hitsu* with a seal *Hogyoku*.
By courtesy of the Victoria and Albert Museum.

8 Utagawa Sadatora (working circa 1825–1860).
Convolvulus and other flowers by the light of the moon. Colour print from wood blocks. Signed *Gototei Sadatora ga*. 1855.
By courtesy of the Victoria and Albert Museum. Photo: Ian Thomas

9 Ando Hiroshige (1797–1858).
Evening rain at Eitai bridge, from a series of views of Edo (modern Tokyo). This atmospheric print is one of Hiroshige's most famous exercises in the fan format. Colour print from wood blocks.
Signed *Hiroshige ga*. circa 1846.
By courtesy of the Victoria and Albert Museum.

10 Katsukawa Shunsho (1726–1792) and Ippitsusai Buncho (working circa 1765–1792).
Double page spread from *Ehon Butai Ogi* ('Picture book of fans for the stage'), published in three volumes in 1770.
This very popular work exemplifies the style of Shunsho and Buncho, which had a revolutionary effect on the development of the actor print. The inscriptions, restored by a later hand, give the names of the actors. Colour prints from wood blocks.
By courtesy of the Victoria and Albert Museum.

11, 12, 13

Box and *inro* (miniature medicine case carried from the waist), lacquered wood, and a *tsuba* (sword guard), copper and other metals. Three examples showing the stylized use of the fan motif in the applied arts. The theme of 'scattered fans' which appears on the *inro* and the *tsuba* has been popular since the fourteenth century.
By courtesy of the Victoria and Albert Museum.

Plate captions continued on page 25

PLATE 1

PLATE 2

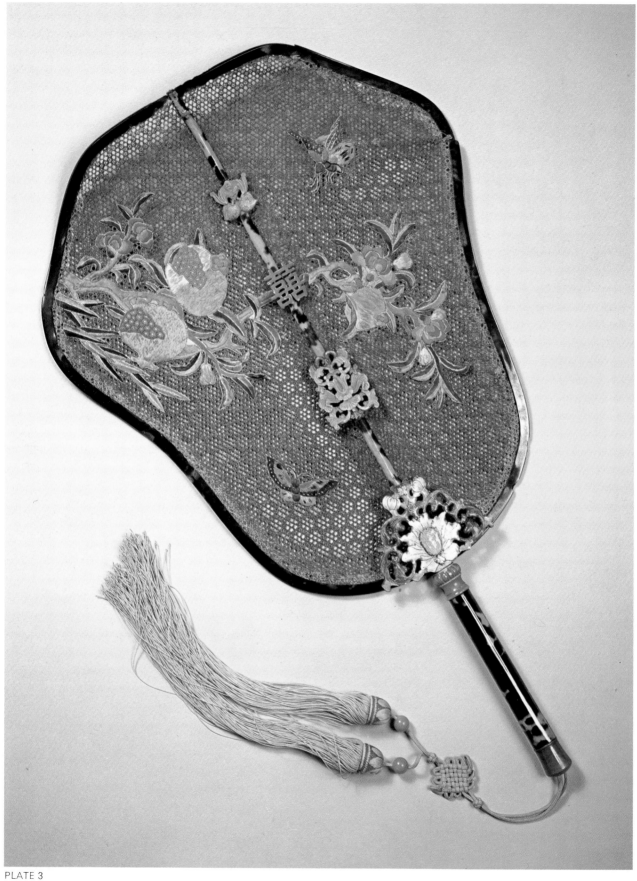

PLATE 3

PLATE 4

PLATE 5

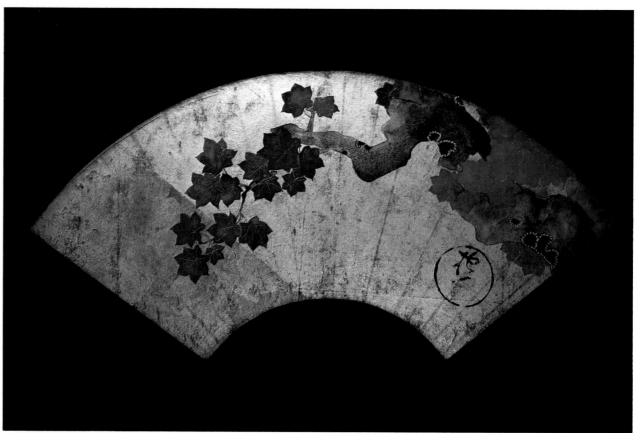

PLATE 6

PLATE 7

PLATE 8

PLATE 9

PLATE 10

PLATE 11

PLATE 12

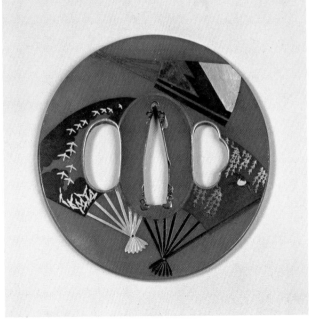

PLATE 13

PLATE 14

PLATE 15

PLATE 16

PLATE 17

PLATE 18

PLATE 19

PLATE 20

PLATE 21

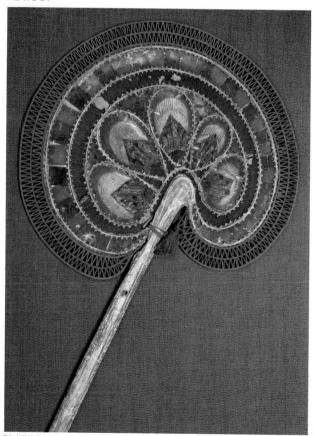

PLATE 22

PLATE 23

PLATE 24

PLATE 25

22

PLATE 26

PLATE 27

PLATE 28

PLATE 29

Captions to colour plates continued from page 8

Chapter 3

14 Painting in watercolours of the interior of a warehouse for the
East India Market. Originally a fan. Possibly Dutch,
circa 1770–1820
By courtesy of the Victoria and Albert Museum.

15 Fan, paper leaf with a *Chinoiserie* scene painted in watercolours
with insertions of mica and appliqué straw and feathers. The sticks
of ivory, the panaches of painted wood and appliqué feathers.
Possibly Dutch, third quarter of the eighteenth century.
From the Messel Collection: by courtesy of the Countess of Rosse.

16 Fan, vellum leaf painted in watercolours with *Chinoiserie* figures
with appliqué ivory faces and silk costumes on either side of a
hand coloured aquatint of three female figures representing the
Arts by Angelica Kauffman. Other appliqué decoration consists of
stamped paper flowers and straw leaves. The sticks are of carved
and pierced ivory. The guards are set with Jasper ware plaques in
gilt mounts. English, circa 1800.
Anonymous collection.

17 Fan, kid leaf painted in watercolours of monochrome green
highlighted with gold paint. The leaf is divided into six asymetrical
compartments showing *Chinoiserie* and European scenes. The
sticks are of carved and pierced ivory with the central pair and
alternate sticks stained ochre and painted with flowers. Possibly
Dutch, circa 1770s.
Anonymous collection.

18 Fan, paper leaf painted in watercolours showing a *Chinoiserie*
scene after the style of Jean-Baptiste Pillement. The painted sticks
are carved and pierced ivory inlaid with silver gilt foil. Possibly
French, mid-eighteenth century.
Anonymous collection.

19 Fan, colour printed cotton satin in Japonaiserie style. English,
late nineteenth century.
By courtesy of George Borchard.

Chapter 4

20 Palm-tree shaped ivory chowrie of the eighteenth century,
probably from Patiala State. Carved with iris and poppy motifs from
traditional Mughal miniatures, with a pineapple finial at the base.
By courtesy of the Victoria and Albert Museum

21 Double crescent-shaped Indian fan of plaited straw entirely
covered with a cotton fabric solidly embroidered with sequins,
gold and silver thread and with blue and red glass beads, the design
of fruit, foliage and peacocks. Lining of multi-coloured striped
silk. Handle of silver. Nineteenth century.
By courtesy of the Victoria and Albert Museum.

22 Lobe-shaped fan from India, nineteenth century. Split bamboo
overlaid with gilt foil. Floral decorations in colour overlaid with
shaped motifs of clear mica. Straight wooden handle.
By courtesy of the Victoria and Albert Museum.

23 Large circular fan made of cotton overlaid with porcupine quills
in floral and circular motifs in red and white with a circle bound with
interwoven coloured straw. Border of peacock feathers. Turned
wooden handle painted red, yellow, and black. Nineteenth century,
from Subsagur in Assam.
By courtesy of the Victoria and Albert Museum.

24 Each of the seven 'sticks' of this brisé fan are made from dried and
pressed loofahs ('cucurbit', a member of the cucumber family) in
the nineteenth century, in Thailand. Above them are fixed duck
feathers, edged with maribou, and with a decoration of red, yellow,
green, and turquoise parokeet feathers.
By courtesy of Martin Willcocks.

25 Folding fan made from natural 'lace-bark' or 'Lagetta Lintearia' tree.
It has a border of Spatha, the sheath of the fruit of the Mountain
Cabbage Palm, the tassel is made from the fibre from the
Pineapple plant. The decoration is dried, pressed ferns, the sticks
of bone and a metal loop. Nineteenth or twentieth century,
from Java.
By courtesy of Martin Willcocks.

26 Green velvet Indian fan. The design is almost the same on the
obverse and the reverse, with silver-covered thread embroidery
showing peacocks and flying fish around a central medallion
which is sewn with silver threads, silver sequins, crystal beads and
pierced red and green stones onto a background of grass-green
velvet; the surround of gold braid and faded gold-covered cotton.
The handle is sewn with the same velvet and two women's heads
at each end, each wearing necklaces and earrings, circa, nineteenth
century.
By courtesy of Martin Willcocks.

Chapter 5

27 'Landscape' (the finished painting of the three stages of technique
on colour)
by Prince P'u Ch'uan

28 The 'Named Fan'
by the Wu brothers

29 The 'Farewell Fan'
by Prince P'u Ch'uan, 1948.

1 Fan painting, ink and slight colour on silk.
Chinese, late twelfth century.
By courtesy of the Trustees of the British Museum.

Chapter 1 Chinese fans and fans from China

Julia Hutt

The vast land mass which constitutes modern China is, by its very nature, subject to extreme climatic variations. Those areas of China which, both in different historical periods and in recent times, have been the most densely populated, have largely coincided with some of the country's hottest regions. The evolution of the fan in China, as an implement with which to agitate the air and thus cool oneself, was no accident. The fan rapidly became an important accessory to Chinese dress, while the decorative surface of the various formats provided endless scope for the creative expression of Chinese artists and craftsmen alike.

Although both men and women in China traditionally used fans, few or no modifications were dictated by the sex of the owner. In court circles, detailed regulations established not only the type of fan to be used during the various seasons of the year, but also the different fans to which each rank of officials was entitled[1]. Thus, it is recorded[2] that 'the Son of Heaven (that is to say, the Emperor) uses feather fans in summer and silk fans in winter'. Outside the court, fashion and function likewise dictated the adoption of various different fans throughout the year by all but the lowest stratum of society. This, however, varied according to the historical period and the geographical location. According to one source[3], folding fans, silk screen fans, and feather fans were used respectively during the first, second and third months of summer, while a poem by Ou-yang Hsiu (1007–72) states that 'In the tenth month the people of the capital turn to their warm fans', that is to say, fans which were suitable for the cooler periods of the year.

The early history of the fan in China is somewhat obscure. The earliest extant examples are probably two woven bamboo side-mounted fans[4] which were excavated from the Ma-wang-tui tomb site near Changsha in Hunan province. They date from the second century BC and are of a degree of sophistication which already suggests a long history even at this early date.

Chinese mythology and literary sources attribute the invention of the fan to various mythological and historical emperors, including Huang Ti, the Emperor Shun and Wu Wang (1027–25 BC). It is also associated with certain legends, the most common of which refers to the Feast of Lanterns[5]. It is more likely, however, that Chinese scholars sought to accord illustrious origins to the fan by linking its invention with certain historical figures. It is also probable that the adoption of the fan was generated by the spontaneous action of ordinary people who used a large leaf or some other suitable object to cool themselves.

Typologically, Chinese fans can be divided into three groups[6]: the screen or rigid fan, the ceremonial fan, and, at a later date, the folding fan. The screen fan, *pien-mien*, was a term applied to any rigid fan which could conveniently be held in the hand and used to agitate the air. The typical screen fan was made either of feathers, or silk, which was frequently painted or embroidered, and which was stretched over a round or oval frame.

The ceremonial fan, which is most commonly referred to as *t'uan-shan* in Chinese sources, differed from the screen fan essentially in that it was of larger proportions and was mounted on a long handle. It was initially used in the ceremonial entourage of high officials and, subsequently, at any important function or procession, together with the ceremonial umbrella and banner. Indeed, the distinction between the ceremonial fan and banner is a difficult one to make for they often served a dual purpose.

In their early history the ceremonial and screen fans were closely connected. Surviving examples before the tenth century, however, are rare and it is necessary to rely on literary references and pictorial representation in paintings, as well as stone reliefs of the second century AD and later. Prior to the Tang dynasty (618–907) the tail feathers of the Reeves pheasant, which was indigenous to North China, were most frequently used in the manufacture of screen and ceremonial fans for the court[7]. During the Tang dynasty, however, pheasant feathers were largely supplanted by the use of the tail feathers of the peacock, which were imported from Annam[8]. It is also interesting to note that, at about this time, various offices of fan-bearers were created and it is recorded, for example, that the officer in charge of the imperial carriages was responsible for the disposition of one hundred and fifty six peacock-tail fans at great state receptions[9]. Economies at court during the eighth century, however, necessitated the introduction of embroidered replicas of peacock-tails or fans composed of a combination of feathers, usually placed round the edge of the fan, with painted or embroidered silk in the centre.

Painted silk fans also appear to have been used from an early date. It is recorded in the biography of Ho Chi in the official Southern Ch'i History that 'the emperor Hsiao Wu (454–464) presented Ho Chi with a fan depicting cicada and sparrow, the work of an expert painter, Ku Ching-hsiu.[10]' Fans decorated with landscape scenes are also thought to have existed at least as early as the fifth century.

It was not, however, until the Sung dynasty (960–1279), and particularly during the reign of the Emperor Hui Tsung (1101–1126), that fan paintings assumed considerable importance both in the history of Chinese fans and as an established branch of Chinese painting (fig. 1). Broadly speaking, artists of the Northern Sung period (960–1127) favoured a monumental style of painting which suggested immense panoramic views. Under the leadership of the Emperor Hui Tsung, and through the Southern Sung period (1127–1279), a more intimate style developed which was admirably suited to the format of the screen fan. The focal point of such paintings was frequently one of the lower corners of the composition or, alternately, the viewer's eye was drawn across the composition by the disposition of elements of the design in diagonally opposing corners. The decoration of the ceremonial fan, however, continued to be symmetrical about a central axis.

The development of the painted screen fan was somewhat

11a Fan box, black and gold lacquer, blue silk and pasteboard interior.
To contain lacquer fan illustrated in figure 11.
Chinese, for the Western market, mid-nineteenth century.
By courtesy of the Victoria and Albert Museum.

Fan case, white satin, embroidered with coloured silk and gilt
paper, blue silk interior.
Chinese, nineteenth century.
By courtesy of the Victoria and Albert Museum.

2 Fan painting, ink and light colours on paper.
Signed Wang Yuan-ch'i (1642–1715).
Chinese, late seventeenth or early eighteenth century.
From a private collection.

curtailed by the appearance of the folding fan in China. The folding fan, *che-shan*, is thought to have originated in Japan and will be discussed more fully in the chapter on Japanese fans. There is, however, discrepancy as to the date of its earliest appearance in China. Isolated literary references indicate that examples of the Japanese folding fan had already reached China as early as the tenth century. A Chinese work, dated 960, states that the folding fan was 'introduced by Tchang-ping-hai[12] and was offered as tribute by barbarians from the southeast who came holding in their hands the pleated fan which occasioned much laughter and ridicule[13].' A Japanese source[14], on the other hand, records that a Chinese priest, Chonen, introduced the folding fan from Japan in 988. By the eleventh century, the Japanese folding fan had already aroused the interest of the Chinese literati, as witnessed by certain comments in their writings[15]. Later, in the fifteenth century, legend states that a folding fan was presented to the Ming emperor Ch'eng Tsu (1403–1424) by Korean ambassadors. He was so impressed with it that he ordered a large quantity to be made for distribution amongst his officials[16]. Chinese tradition, moreover, confirms that the indigenous folding fan with painted decoration did not become widely fashionable until the early fifteenth century. It has even been suggested that, at first the folding fan became popular among prostitutes from the ports of Chekiang, where they came into direct contact with Japanese traders, though it gradually became accepted by men and women of other social ranks[16].

The folding fan was generally composed of a semi-circular leaf of silk or paper, which was pressed into folds. Sticks, which averaged between ten and thirty in number, were then inserted between the folds to form a support. The sticks were commonly of bamboo, the most highly prized being the *hsiang-fei* mottled bamboo from Hunan, and, more rarely, of ivory or sandalwood. When not in use, the folding fan was easily carried in a cloth case (fig. 11a), which was suspended from the belt, or the fan was inserted either in the sleeve or at the back of the neck in the folds of the male dress or, when in full dress, in the boot. This was a distinct advantage over the more cumbersome screen fan. The majority were purchased already decorated. Wealthy people of fashion, together with the literati, however, preferred to buy a plain fan leaf and commission a prestigious artist to paint it. It was also the custom to request an artist to paint a fan for a particular purpose, such as a farewell gift or as a token of friendship.

The format of the folding fan became something of a challenge to Chinese artists from the Ming dynasty onwards and inventive use of the limited surface area was of paramount importance. Fan painting thus became established as a recognized branch of Chinese painting, and the majority of leading artists produced paintings for fans among their works (fig. 2 and plate 4). To follow the development of fan painting from the Ming dynasty onwards, therefore, would largely be to trace the history of Chinese painting during this period. It is also worth mentioning that it was precisely because such paintings were highly prized that they were frequently removed from their frames or sticks and preserved in albums.

Painted screen fans have continued to be made right up to the present day, frequently depicting bird and flower subjects, though they have remained largely outside the mainstream of creative Chinese painting. The most interesting screen fans of subsequent periods, moreover, were those composed of such materials as *k'o-ssu* (woven silk tapestry), and embroidered fabrics (plate 3), which were stretched over frames of varying shape, as well as other more unusual materials, such as jade (fig. 4) or plaited ivory.

When considering the long history of the fan in China and its importance as an object of fashion, it is hardly surprising that certain distinctive types evolved which were characteristic of a particular city or region. Hangchou, for example, was known for a black oiled folding fan, which may have been composed of as many as fifty sticks, and which was decorated with gold splashes. In the province of Chekiang, rigid fans, known as the 'jade-plaque' fan, were carved from the giant bamboo. Another variety, which was frequently termed the 'Swatow' fan from whence it was decorated, was in fact made in the province of Kuangtung. It was composed of a piece of bamboo, which was split into radiating slips about two-thirds along its length. The slips were then arranged and secured in the desired shape and were covered with decorated paper. Of particular interest is the betel palm fan (fig. 3), which was made in Taiwan. After the leaf had been cut into a suitable shape, it was dried and engraved with a hot poker or joss-sticks.

Another curious fan, which was made in both Peking and Canton, was the 'hidden scene' fan (plate 1). Such a fan, when opened in the normal custom from left to right, revealed scenes of an innocuous nature. When opened from right to left, however, the viewer was presented with a titillating or pornographic scene. There were also examples of fans for both tourists and travellers which depicted topographical guides or printed maps (fig. 5), which were adapted to the shape of the fan.

The eighteenth century witnessed a considerable development in trade between China and the West. Apart from such commodities as tea, sugar and silk, an increasingly large proportion of Chinese exports included fancy goods such as fans and fan sticks. These were mostly exported in bulk for wholesale distribution in Europe and America by public auction, though certain articles were commissioned by specific shops or individuals. In the latter case, fans which date from approximately 1780 to 1815 frequently portrayed the owner's monogram incorporated into the design (fig. 10). Sailors were also permitted to carry a certain quantity of goods in their personal luggage and it is probable that a significant number of Chinese fans reached Europe in this way. Canton was the centre of trade with Europe (fig. 6), together with Macao and Hong Kong at a later date.

As the eighteenth century progressed, Europe witnessed an increasing interest in China, which manifested itself partly in a desire for objects of Chinese manufacture. The Chinese sought to exploit this ready market by supplying the West with goods of a directly popular appeal. This was achieved by evolving a style of decoration which adapted traditional Chinese motifs and combined them to a greater or lesser extent with elements of Western design.

Fans which were exported to the West were thus of a distinctive type and were rarely used by the Chinese. They were composed of a wide variety of materials, such as gold and silver filigree, cloisonné enamel, lacquer and kingfisher feathers, to mention but a few. Fans composed entirely of such materials were necessarily of the brisé type, that is, they were composed of individual sticks of a rigid material, which were joined together by means of a ribbon or thread. Although the brisé fan was made in China for the Western market from the eighteenth century onwards (fig. 9), it does not appear to have achieved any degree of popularity among the Chinese. During the nineteenth century there was also a general tendency towards novel designs and shapes which were previously unknown in China, such as the cockade and asymmetric fan.

Although Chinese fans were exported to the West as early as the seventeenth century, surviving examples from the period are few in number. Probably the earliest fans to be made specifically for the Western market which form a distinctive group are a number of ivory fans (fig. 8). They were small in size and were of a wedge shape which was dictated by contemporary European fashion. Fans of this type were characterized by painted designs, which were of Chinese or Western inspiration, or a combination of both, against a background of pierced ivory. A striking feature of this group of fans was the similarity of their painted decoration to contemporary styles of Chinese porcelain, particularly those which were already favoured by the Western market, such as *famille verte* and so-called 'Chinese Imari'. This may be explained partly as an attempt to decorate fans for the Western market in styles of decoration which were already familiar and acceptable in another medium.

Although fans of this type were no longer made after around 1730, little is known about fans for the West until the latter part of the eighteenth century. Ivory continued to be the most widely used material in the manufacture of fans, though the proportions of these fans were generally larger. In many cases, painted decoration disappeared altogether or was reduced to small panels, while the pierced ivory itself became the focal point in the overall decorative scheme. The ivory was pierced with designs of flowers or geometric designs of a highly sophisticated nature, against which roundels, shaped panels and, above all, a central shield were portrayed. The influence of neo-classical designs also became increasingly evident (fig. 7). Towards the end of the eighteenth century the most striking innovation was the appearance of a ribbed ground, at first confined to small areas, but gradually covering the entire surface area of the fan. This was also accompanied by the introduction of isolated architectural, landscape and floral elements in the overall design. It was, however, above all, the decoration of the guards with a distinctive design of scrolling flowers which served to distinguish the aforementioned fans (fig. 7).

By the early nineteenth century, the decoration of ivory fans came to be dominated by carved figures in architectural or landscape settings on a ribbed ground. At first, a few figures only were portrayed. Gradually, however, greater emphasis was placed on filling the entire surface area with a profusion of small figures and other motifs, which bore no apparent relationship to the shape of the fan. At the same time, the fan itself became smaller, the sticks thicker and the carving cruder, while the decoration was frequently confined to one side of the fan only (fig. 9). The above chronology of styles also applies to materials other than ivory, such as mother-of-pearl, sandalwood and tortoise-shell, though such examples were less common. It is also worth noting that ivory, as well as lacquer, was frequently used in the manufacture of sticks and guards for fan leaves of a different material (fig. 6).

Black and gold lacquer brisé fans constituted a large proportion of Chinese fans made for the Western market. The earliest lacquer fans, which date from approximately 1790 to 1820, were small in size and composed of comparatively thick sticks. They were decorated with a continuous design of the vine-leaf motif or a scrolling leaf pattern, against which a shield, enclosing the owner's monogram, was frequently portrayed (fig. 10). During the 1820s, figure and architectural subjects were also introduced into the decorative repertoire of the lacquer fan.

Towards the middle of the nineteenth century, the lacquer fan became larger and the sticks thinner, while there was a tendency towards designs of an ornate and detailed nature, which were almost identical on both sides of the fan (fig. 11). Another type of fan, which dates from around 1820 onwards, combined lacquer sticks with a painted panel executed in either bold colours (fig. 12) or colours resembling the different tones of gold lacquer.

Boxes designed to contain and complement fans for the Western market were frequently composed of lacquer (fig. 11a) or of pasteboard covered with fabric. Generally speaking, the fan and the fan box were of equally high quality, and both formed an integral part of the finished product.

There was a striking difference between painted fans, which were executed by Chinese artists working in traditional styles, and craftsmen who added painted decoration to fans for the Western market. The latter were essentially professional painters who were grouped together in workshops and studios. They worked partly in a traditional style of painting which was characteristic of the Chinese craftsman and professional painter[17] and were partly influenced by Western painting. Some painters possibly came into direct contact with artists working in the Western manner through Jesuit missionaries, such as Giuseppe Castiglione (1688–1768), as well as official ship's painters from Europe and America. The interest in western painting was further encouraged by the arrival of George Chinnery in Canton in 1825 and by his subsequent success and popularity as an artist.

Fan paintings for the Western market can be divided into three types: those which wholly imitated scenes of Western inspiration, those which depicted scenes of Chinese life, and those which were a combination of the two. Fan paintings of Western inspiration were often difficult to distinguish from their European counterparts. They were, however, generally characterized by a somewhat clumsy and awkward depiction of the subject matter, particularly with regard to costume and physique, for these were largely beyond the experience and

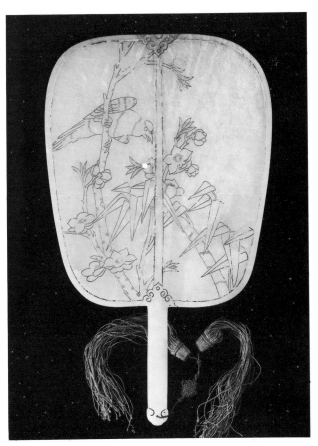

3 Rigid fan, betel palm, engraved with a hot poker or joss-sticks.
   Chinese, mid or late nineteenth century.
   By courtesy of the Horniman Museum.

4 Screen fan, jade with gilt decoration.
   Reverse inscribed with a poem.
   Chinese, reign mark and seal of Ch'ien Lung (1736–95).
   This fan was probably intended for ceremonial use.
   By courtesy of the Fitzwilliam Museum.

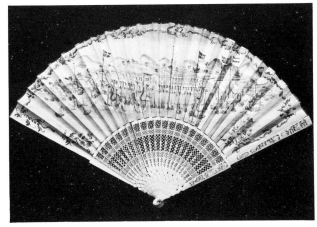

5 Folding fan, printed paper, bamboo sticks.
   Inscribed *tsui-hsin Che-chiang sheng-ch'eng ch'üan-t'u*, 'the
   latest complete map of the provincial capital of Chekiang (that is to
   say, Hangchou).'
   Reverse with topographical guide of the West Lake.
   Chinese, late nineteenth or early twentieth century.
   By courtesy of Martin Willcocks.

6 Folding fan, painted paper leaf, pierced ivory sticks.
   The waterfront at Canton with *hongs* for the
   Western merchants.
   Reverse with three sprays of flowers.
   Chinese, for the Western market, second half 18th century.
   This is a typical example of a group of fans which date from this
   period. They are characterized by ivory sticks pierced with
   geometric designs, three floral sprays on one side of the fan leaf and
   a painted scene, frequently depicting birds and flowers, on the other.
   By courtesy of the Victoria and Albert Museum.

7 Brisé fan, pierced and carved ivory.
Chinese, for the Western market, late eighteenth century.
This fan portrays a combination of neo-classical elements, landscape and architectural scenes and floral motifs on a ribbed ground. The guards are carved with scrolling flowers.
By courtesy of the Merseyside County Museums.

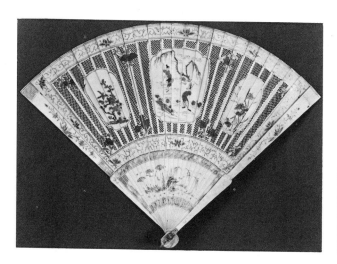

8 Brisé fan, ivory, pierced and painted in colours and gilt.
Chinese, for the Western market, early eighteenth century.
This fan imitates 'Chinese Imari' style porcelain with a predominance of blue, red and, above all, gilt.
By the courtesy of the Victoria and Albert Museum.

9 Brisé fan, carved ivory.
Chinese, for the Western market, circa 1830.
This fan is carved on one side only.
By courtesy of the Victoria and Albert Museum.

10 Brisé fan, black and gold lacquer.
Vine-leaf motif with scrolling leaf borders.

Chinese, for the Western market, early nineteenth century.
By courtesy of Bertha de Vere Green.

understanding of the Chinese professional painter (see cover). In such cases, the painter was working from sketches, designs and, more particularly, prints, many of which had been sent to China as models for the decoration of porcelain for the Western market.

Scenes portraying the domestic, social and ceremonial life of China were extremely popular in the West. Fans decorated with such scenes were also no exception (figs. 12 and 15). At the same time, paintings depicting various Chinese trades and occupations, which were frequently grouped together to form an album, were greatly admired. These provide us with certain visual records as to the various stages in the manufacture of Chinese fans during the late eighteenth and nineteenth centuries (figs. 13 and 79).

Perhaps the most common subject for the painted decoration of fans was the depiction of flowers, fruit, birds and insects (plate 2). Such designs were frequently bold in conception, vivid in colour and, when executed on paper, were often on a gold or silver ground (fig. 14).

It has already been noted how the feather fan played a significant role in the history of Chinese fans. Whereas feather fans for the Chinese were of the rigid variety, fans for the Western market were usually of the brisé type. Certain feather fans of the latter variety, such as those made from the feathers of the Argos pheasant, relied entirely on the natural pattern and coloration of the feathers for their decoration. Others, particularly those composed of goose feathers, were enhanced by painted designs executed in gouache. These were mostly akin to painted silk and paper fans, with designs of flowers, fruit, birds and insects predominating.

Another interesting type of fan is that which is frequently termed the 'mandarin' or 'one hundred faces' fan. It was characterized by a varying number of figures composed of silk robes and painted ivory faces, which were applied to the painted fan leaf. As it is precisely this element which serves to distinguish such fans, it would, perhaps, be more appropriate to describe them as 'applied figure' fans.

The nineteenth century applied figure fan may be considered as a logical development from a group of fans which date from the second half of the eighteenth century (fig. 37). They were composed of applied materials such as mica, straw, feathers and, above all, silk, which was frequently used to depict the human figure, as in the later applied figure fan. It would seem highly likely that this novel method of fan decoration was influenced partly by lacquer furniture decorated with encrustations of semi-precious stones and, above all, by bone and feather pictures of the Ch'ien Lung period (1736–95)[18].

Chinese applied figure fans of the early nineteenth century portrayed figures which rarely exceeded fifteen in number (fig. 15), and which were generally of secondary importance in the overall design. Towards the 1820s, the applied figures were portrayed in increasingly large numbers, together with greater attention to minute detail. Applied figure fans con-

11 Brisé fan, black and gold lacquer.
Chinese, for the Western market, mid-nineteenth century.
By courtesy of the Victoria and Albert Museum.

12 Brisé fan, painted and lacquered.
Chinese, for the Western market, early nineteenth century.
From a private collection.

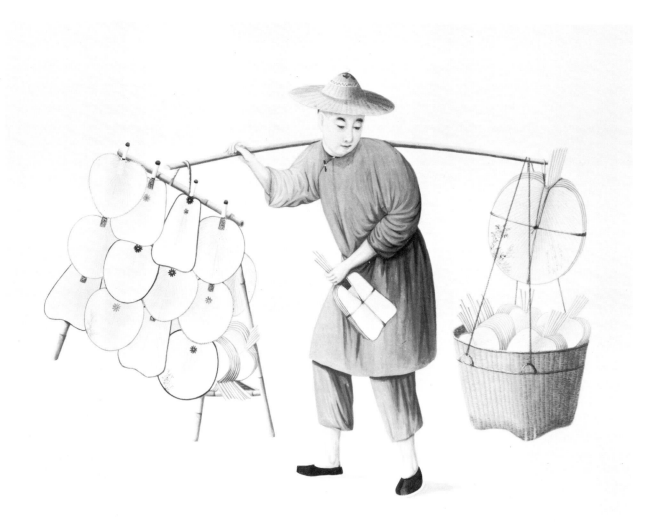

13 Watercolour on paper, depicting a fan seller, one of a set of a
hundred paintings portraying various trades and occupations.

Chinese, for the Western market, nineteenth century.
By courtesy of the Victoria and Albert Museum.

14 Folding fan, painted paper on a golden ground, gilt ivory sticks. Chinese, for the Western market, early nineteenth century. The reverse is illustrated in fig. 15. *By courtesy of Martin Willcocks.*

15 Folding fan, applied figures on painted paper, gilt ivory sticks. Chinese, for the Western market, early nineteenth century. The reverse is illustrated in fig. 14. *By courtesy of Martin Willcocks.*

tinued to be made in this manner almost unchanged until the end of the nineteenth century. Their enormous popularity in Europe and America may be explained partly as answering the demand for fans of an ingenious and unusual type.

In Europe and many other countries of the world, the vicissitudes of fashion have long since resulted in the disappearance of the fan from everyday use. In parts of China, however, the fan is still widely used during the hot summer months, for practical considerations rather than as an object of fashion, though this in itself does not preclude its decoration. Fans, which are based on traditional materials and designs, have thus continued to be manufactured in China today in specialist workshops and factories.

Notes

1 In the *Huang-ch'ao li-ch'i t'u-shih* (The Illustrated Catalogue of Ritual Paraphernalia of the Ching Dynasty), numbers 900–1896, 901 & A-1896, 903 & A-1896 of the copy at the Victoria and Albert Museum refer to ceremonial fans for use by different ranks. For example, 903A–1896 states: 'The circular screen borne by the Guard of an Imperial Concubine is carefully designed in accordance with the Imperial order issued in the fourteenth year of the reign of Ch'ien Lung (1749). It is made of red-clouded satin and is in all other respects identical with the circular screen borne by the Guard of Imperial Concubines of the first rank.'
2 Quoting from *Hsi-ching tsa-chi* in *San-ts'ai t'u-hui*, Ming edition compiled by Wang Ch'i and Wang Ssu-i, chuan 107, page 16.
3 John Hay, *An Exhibition of the Art of Chinese Fan Painting*, Milne Henderson Gallery 1974, Introduction.
4 *Ch'ang-sha Ma-wang-tui i-hao Han-mu*, Peking 1974, volume II, pls. 229 & 234.
5 G. W. Whooliscroft Rhead, *History of the Fan*, London, 1910, page 46.
6 This typology excludes the mechanical fan, which is somewhat beyond the scope of this article. For a full description see Joseph Needham, *Science and Civilization in China*, volume IV:2, Cambridge, 1965.
7 Edward H. Schafer, *The Golden Peaches of Samarkand*, California, 1963, page 111.
8 Ibid. pages 111-112.
9 Ibid. page 112.
10 John Hay, *Chinese Fan Painting, in Chinese Painting and the Decorative Style*, in *Colloquies on Art and Archaeology in Asia no. 5*, Percival David Foundation, London, 1975, page 101.
11 Ibid., page 101.
12 The name has been left in the romanization used by G. W. Whooliscroft Rhead as he does not quote a Chinese source and the characters are, therefore, not known.
13 Whooliscroft Rhead, op. cit., page 52.
14 Noma Seiroku, *Soshingu*, in *Nihon no Bijutsu* no. 1, Tokyo, 1967.
15 John Hay, *Chinese Fan Painting*, op. cit., pages 106–7.
16 *San-ts'ai t'u-hui*, Ming edition compiled by Wang Ch'i and Wang Ssu-i, chuan 78, page 41.
17 Paintings executed by Chinese craftsmen and professional painters were frequently of similar style and composition to Chinese architectural decorations (as illustrated in *Chung-kuo chen-chu ts'ai-hua t'u-an*, Peking, 1955) and Chinese popular woodblock prints (as illustrated in Alekseeyev Vasily Mikhailovich, *Kitaiskaya Narodnava Kartina*, Moscow, 1966).
18 For examples see Setterwall, Fogelmarck, Gyllensvärd, *The Chinese Pavilion at Drottningholm*, Malmö, 1974, pages 200–202.

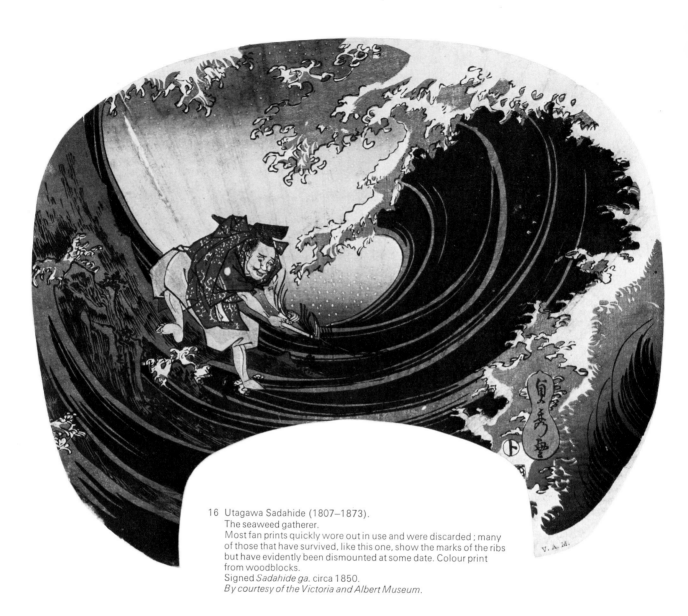

16 Utagawa Sadahide (1807–1873).
The seaweed gatherer.
Most fan prints quickly wore out in use and were discarded ; many
of those that have survived, like this one, show the marks of the ribs
but have evidently been dismounted at some date. Colour print
from woodblocks.
Signed *Sadahide ga*. circa 1850.
By courtesy of the Victoria and Albert Museum.

Chapter 2 The fan in Japan

Joe Earle

Deep inside a burial mound of the sixth century AD in Fukuoka prefecture on the island of Kyushu may be found what are probably the earliest representations of fans in Japanese art. The end wall of the tumulus is decorated in black and ochre with a curious composition of breaking waves, boats, horses and a human figure, flanked by two upright poles, each bearing at its end a large oval shape covered with radiating stripes. These ovals are without any doubt fans.

The tumulus culture of Japan (third to sixth century AD) was permeated with Chinese influences absorbed via Korea and the fans in this painting bear a marked resemblance to those we see in Chinese depictions of ceremonial processions dating from the Later Han dynasty (25–220 AD). The radiating stripes are evidently intended to represent the feathers from which these fans, like their Chinese counterparts, were made.

Further evidence for the early history of the fan is provided by a painting discovered at Takamatsuzuka burial mound near the old city of Nara in 1972. This painting, in early Chinese T'ang dynasty (618–906) style and of late seventh or early eighth century date, shows female courtiers, one of whom carries a circular screen fan of Chinese type, probably made from fabric, on a long stick.

The first surviving Japanese example of a fan-like object is to be found among the vast collections assembled around 756 in the Shosoin, a storehouse attached to the great Todaiji temple at Nara, then capital of Japan. The Nara period (646–794) is characterized by strong Chinese influences and among the many items of Chinese manufacture or Chinese inspiration in the Shosoin there is a curious object called the *jinbi*, a stick attached to two vertical strips of wood between which are fastened a large number of animal hairs. The overall shape is an upright half-oval. The continental origin of this piece is confirmed by a near identical eighth-century example painted in the caves of Tun Huang in north-western China. Like the tumulus period fans, the *jinbi* was probably more a symbol of rank and a ceremonial object than a practical instrument for creating a breeze.

Narrative scrolls painted at the end of the Heian period (794–1185) indicate that circular or near-circular Chinese-style screen fans were still in use during the twelfth century and that the lower orders were cooling themselves with simple fans made from woven straw or similar material. The same scrolls also show us that the screen fan had already yielded in popularity to the two types of folding fan developed during the Heian period. These are Japan's most important contribution to the world of the fan. They are the *hiogi* ('cypress fan'), equivalent to the European brisé fan, and the folding paper fan. The *hiogi* is made up of a number of thin strips of wood, usually cypress, which are pierced at one end and held together by a rivet while a thread at the other end controls the maximum spread. The paper fan, called the 'bat fan' in many Heian period sources, is made up of a number of sticks, similarly pierced, to which a piece of paper is stuck on one side.

The evidence in favour of a Japanese origin for the folding fan is circumstantial rather than conclusive, but contemporary sources suggest that the fan was popular in Japan long before it became widespread on the mainland and there was certainly nothing resembling the *hiogi*, rather than the paper fan, in China until a much later date. The Japanese case is not helped by romantic stories about the invention of the folding fan which have been popular among Europeans in the past. These relate to the paper fan rather than the *hiogi*. According to one, a man named Toyo-maru from Tamba province made one after being inspired by the sight of a bat's wing at some time during the reign of the semi-legendary Empress Jingo (r. 201–269). Another account tells the same story but transfers it to an anonymous artisan working during the late seventh century. A third source has it that the widow of Taira no Atsumori (d. 1184), who retired to a temple in Kyoto, cured its abbot of a fever by fanning him with a hastily improvised fan made from a folded piece of paper and thereby made the discovery accidentally. Yet another individual credited with the invention is the Emperor Gosanjo (r. 1068–1072), who is supposed to have created the first folding paper fan when he repaired a broken *hiogi* by sticking paper to it. The mutually contradictory nature of these tales should in itself suffice to dismiss them as mere fictions. The real evidence for Japanese fan history, which consists of actual examples, depictions in other works of art and Japanese and Chinese literary references, tells a different story.

One modern Japanese writer[1] has suggested, as a likely precursor of the *hiogi*, objects known as *mokkan* – thin pieces of wood about 30 cms long and 4 or 5 cms wide – which were widely used during the Nara period by court officials as a kind of notebook. Large numbers bearing a wide variety of random jottings and inscriptions have been excavated and the folding fan may perhaps owe its origin to some enterprising bureaucrat who, in order to keep his bundle of *mokkan* tidy, pierced them at one end and held them together with a rivet or a thread. Not long ago during restoration work at the Toji temple in Kyoto (the imperial capital during the Heian period) there were found inside an image of Kannon (the Buddhist goddess of mercy) twenty slips of wood which could be the remains of one of the world's earliest folding fans. No rivet or thread was found and the slips of wood do not taper towards one end, as they do in later *hiogi*, nor can they be arranged in such a way that the sketches and written notes which they bear carry over from one slip to the next; but each is pierced at one end with two holes such as would allow the passage of a thread and the ratio of width to length (1:10) is more typical of the blades of a *hiogi* than a *mokkan* (ratio approximately 1:6). Perhaps we shall never know whether these pieces of wood, one of which is inscribed with a date corresponding to 877, are *mokkan* of a peculiar form, the remains of a *hiogi*, or an example of a transitional stage between the two.

In 894 the Heian government suspended official relations with China and from that time on the life of the court began to be less dominated by Chinese cultural influences. One hundred years later the paper fan was already widely used and it seems likely that the invention of this curious implement was a product of the ever-increasing sophistication and elaboration of costume and manners which typifies Japanese court life of the tenth century. Our first scrap of evidence for the use of the paper fan is to be found on a box for the storage of *sutras* (Buddhist scriptures) which was formerly in the same Toji temple and which was probably made during the early years of the tenth century. It is decorated with paintings showing courtiers playing with a ball; two of these hold what could just be folded fans. If so, they are of a type usual in the later Heian period and known to us from scroll paintings: the paper is stuck to one side of the sticks only and the sticks are thin, with the outer ones no thicker than the rest as was customary at a later date.

A Japanese dictionary[2] compiled during the 930s, which lists both *ogi* and *uchiwa*, offers the first literary evidence. The term *ogi* has since come to refer to the folding fan as opposed to the screen fan, or *uchiwa*, and the compiler may perhaps have intended some contrast between the two.

Firm confirmation of the existence of Japanese folding fans during the tenth century is found in the official history of the Chinese Sung dynasty (960–1280). In the section devoted to Japan, it is recorded that in the year 988 a Japanese monk called Chonen presented some objects at court (visits of this type continued in spite of the official diplomatic break) including twelve *hiogi*[3] and two 'bat fans' which were contained in a special gold and silver lacquered box. Clearly Chonen, who was in China to collect Buddhist images and sculptures, would have wanted to present items which he felt would be new and unusual, but we cannot be certain that folding fans had not been made in China before that date. Japanese fans continued to excite Chinese interest during the eleventh century. A history of painting and kindred matters written around 1074[4] mentions that embassies from Korea used to bring with them folding fans decorated with paintings of people, birds and flowers and these are described as Japanese. Some Chinese writers of this time are obviously confused as to whether the fans they describe are Japanese or Korean, but this is hardly surprising when we consider Korea's importance as a cultural bridge between the two nations.

The popularity of fans is evident from the sumptuary edicts promulgated during the Choho reign period (999–1003) which imposed restrictions on the decoration of both *hiogi* and 'bat fans' but our most comprehensive sources for their decoration and function are two great literary works completed in the early eleventh century, the *Tale of Genji* by Lady Murasaki Shikibu and the *Pillow Book*, a collection of anecdotes and opinions by Lady Sei Shonagon. Courtiers, it appears, were accustomed to commission artists to paint their fans and among those described is one decorated with a tall grove, another with a misty moon reflected in water and another with a traveller's lodging on one side and the capital in a rain storm on the other. Others, we learn, were left unpainted. Fan frames (called *hone*, 'bones') were admired

for themselves and the fastidious Sei Shonagon expresses precise opinions on the right combination of frame and paper: 'blue paper suits a red frame, purple paper suits a green frame'[5].

In the court life of the time the fan served many purposes: it was used to beat time to music, to hide the face when embarrassed or to allow oneself to laugh more freely, to give and receive objects (no doubt it was a useful extension of the hands given the enormous sleeves fashionable at the time), to shade the eyes from the sun and (although this is rarely mentioned) to cool oneself. Poems were written on them, they were exchanged by lovers, they were given as farewell presents and used by dancers and there were even 'fan matches' in which, it seems, the object of the competition was the poems written on the fans rather than the fans themselves. Fans, then, carried by both men and women, were a vital decorative and practical adjunct to aristocratic life. Their use was governed, in theory at least, by a series of regulations concerning the different colours of fans borne by the Emperor and the various ranks of the nobility. 'As I looked at all the men gathered there with their fans', enthuses Sei Shonagon, 'I had the impression that I was seeing a field of pinks in full bloom'[6].

With the illustrated picture scrolls of the twelfth century, mentioned earlier, we have our first reliable body of artistic rather than literary evidence. We can see that paper fans had from about six to about nine sticks[7], with paper on one side only and no specially wide guard sticks at either end. The spread of the fans was small – never more than about ninety degrees. In most cases the small scale and sometimes poor state of preservation of these scrolls make it impossible for us to tell what the designs on the fans were like but there are a few where they can be dimly made out. One is decorated with a large silver moon on a black ground, another has pines on a silver ground and on another is a scene of pines by the shore. The earliest surviving folding paper fans also date from the twelfth century but, as might be expected, they are in a fragmentary state. One, recently discovered in one of the many mounds in which Buddhist scriptures were buried at this time, still retains on its sticks a few scraps of paper decorated with silver and painted with what may be a willow[8].

Much evidence on paper fans has come to us from some rather unusual pieces which have survived from the end of the twelfth century. These are the ninety-eight pieces of fan-shaped paper on which sections of the famous Buddhist scripture, the *Lotus Sutra*, are written over a ground decorated with small squares of gold and silver leaf and painted in rich colours, mainly with figure subjects, although there are also a few landscapes. As with many decorative *sutras* produced during the late Heian and early Kamakura (1185–1392) periods, the painting bears no relation to the text. We cannot tell whether these fan papers were actually intended for use but we do know from the fact that the designs were built up from small woodblocks placed in a series of stereotyped combinations that folding fans, which by their nature last for only a short time if used regularly, were already being produced by what might be termed mass-production techniques. The *Lotus Sutra* fan papers

17 Tani Buncho (1763–1840).
River and willows. In spite of the Chinese allusion in the inscription this painting owes far less to mainland traditions of painting than the landscape, also by Buncho, reproduced below. The soft brushwork of the rain-soaked willow and the placing of the lone fisherman and the opposite shore are pure Japanese. Ink on paper. Signed *a painting of the rainy river south of the Yangtze by Buncho* on the 22nd day of the second month of 1800 with seals *Bun*, *cho*.
Reproduced by courtesy of the Trustees of the British Museum.

18 Tani Buncho (1763–1840). Chinese landscape.
Although he is generally regarded as a *Nanga* artist, Buncho had studied all the types of painting current in his day and his style is highly eclectic. However, in this classic Chinese landscape, with its secluded temple towards which a pilgrim and his attendant make their way over a bridge beneath lofty mountains, we sense the strong influence of Chinese scholar painting which is one hallmark of the *Nanga* style. Ink and colours on paper. Signed *painted by Buncho in the autumn of 1808 at the mountain-drawing-pavilion* with seals *Sha*, *zan*.
From the collection of R. A. Harari, OBE.

19 Onishi Chinnen (1792–1851). Mount Fuji.
This painting of Fuji above the clouds, quickly sketched, we may imagine, at the request of a friend, exemplifies the very essence of the Shijo manner. Ink on paper. Signed *Chinnen* with a gourd-shaped seal *Sonan*.
By courtesy of the Ashmolean Museum, Oxford.

20 Totoki Baigai (1749–1804).
Pike among water plants, with an inscription : 'Outside the city walls there's an odd fish. I don't know its name.' Ink and slight colours on paper. Signed *Baigai* with two seals *Bai, Gai*.
By courtesy of Dennis Wiseman.

are of interest too in that they show us how at this early date the Japanese genius for composition, especially in awkward shapes, had been applied to the fan shape. For one thing, the columns of the text follow the radii of the fan and the characters get smaller the nearer they come to the lower edge of the paper. But more striking still is the composition of the underpainting. All figures, trees, architectural uprights and other elements which would normally be placed vertically are, like the text, arranged to follow the radii of the fan and the horizon and the ground on which the figures stand follow the curves of imaginary circles with their centres at the same point as the centre of the fan itself. It is as if both text and paintings had originally been executed on a rectangle which has then been distorted into the fan shape. The surrealistic impression conveyed by this technique is well suited to the ideal world which these *sutra* paintings aim to portray.

Our evidence for the form and decoration of *hiogi* at this date comes from a small number of examples which have been preserved in shrines at Itsukushima, near Hiroshima, and at other places. Three of the Itsukushima *hiogi* are half the normal size (about 16 cms radius) and are traditionally said to have belonged to the child emperor Antoku who perished in the sea battle of Dannoura in 1185. The Itsukushima fans have thirty-four or thirty-five blades and the surface is treated with *gofun* (powdered white lead) and mica, over which are painted a few rows of trees and flowers on isolated patches of ground with here and there a group of courtiers hunting or playing musical instruments. Another example at the same shrine is decorated with gold and silver leaf and gold dust as well as *gofun* and mica and shows a man, woman and child amid pines and grasses. The style resembles that of scroll paintings of the same date, but as in the *Lotus Sutra* fan leaves the artists have taken full account of the shape. The narrow patches of ground follow the curve of the outline and the trees are placed parallel to the edges of the blades.

The principal changes in the construction of the folding fan during the thirteenth and fourteenth centuries concern the sticks, which increase in size and number and are for the first time decorated with pierced carvings. Carved sticks can be seen on some of the later scrolls[9], but a large part of our knowledge of the fan during the Kamakura period comes from the motif of 'scattered fans' which decorates a well-known lacquer box of the early 14th century[10]. All the fans shown illustrate landscape scenes, mostly with a few trees, flowers, or reeds and the occasional crane, and since these are merely representations of fans in another, decorative, medium, the designs are rather stylized.

The Muromachi period (1392–1568) saw renewed contact with China and Korea which brought about some fundamental developments in fan construction. In China, the folding fan had been pursuing an independent line of development for some time and it was during the Muromachi period that Chinese fans were first introduced to Japan. Their most unusual feature to Japanese eyes was the presence of paper on both sides of the sticks and the increased thickness led to a number of technical problems which resulted in two new forms, the *suehiro* ('wide ended') fan and the *bonbori* fan.

The outer sticks of the former type bend outwards from the middle and, as the name suggests, allow the paper part to open out when it is closed, while those of the latter type bend inwards and hold the thick folds of paper firmly together.

The *uchiwa* or screen fan also changed during this period: the old types of Chinese origin began to give way to the Korean model, in which a large number of bamboo splints emanating from the top of the handle are held between two sheets of paper.

The well-known *gunsen* ('war-fan') makes its first appearance at this time, not so much as a weapon, as is commonly thought, but as a durable instrument (the sticks are of iron) with which to give signals during battle. It should not be confused with another type of the same name, made from paper and lacquered sticks, which was a decorative accoutrement used for parade purposes with the ornate armours of the eighteenth and nineteenth centuries. The *gumpai uchiwa*, a characteristically-shaped stiff fan which is still used by umpires at *sumo* wrestling matches, also owes its origins to the late Muromachi period.

The almost continual warfare of the fifteenth and sixteenth centuries was brought to an end by Tokugawa Ieyasu (1542–1616). The régime of the Tokugawa family lasted until 1868 and brought to Japan a peace and unity it had not known for half a millenium. This stability encouraged the development of trade, the growth of great commercial centres at places like Edo (now Tokyo) and Osaka and the rise of a merchant class which, deprived by a rigid hierarchy of the possibility of using its new wealth to improve itself socially, created a distinctive culture of its own. The life of this urban society is well known to us from the prints and paintings of the *ukiyoe* school, which used for its subject matter (among other things) the world of the theatres and the licensed quarters, and from these we can tell that during the Tokugawa period the use of the folding fan had extended, at least in the towns, to every class.

The varieties which had developed in the preceding centuries continued and apart from the introduction of a number of new shapes of *uchiwa* there are no important changes.

The opening of Japan to the West around the middle of the nineteenth century resulted in an explosion of commercial and industrial activity which was not without its effect on the fan. Vast quantities were exported – over fifteen million were sold abroad in 1891 alone. This colossal export trade caused a catastrophic decline in quality and taste from which the Japanese fan has never recovered.

It will have been noticed that since we cited a lacquer box of the early fourteenth century there has been no mention of the decoration on fans. This omission is deliberate, for it was not long after that time that fan painting came into its own, both in China and in Japan, as a special category of painting to which even the most distinguished artists turned their hands and so it has remained until this century. As a result the painting of fans, apart from *hiogi* and other special types which continued to be decorated in more or less the same way, becomes more a part of the general history of painting than a special aspect of the development of fans.

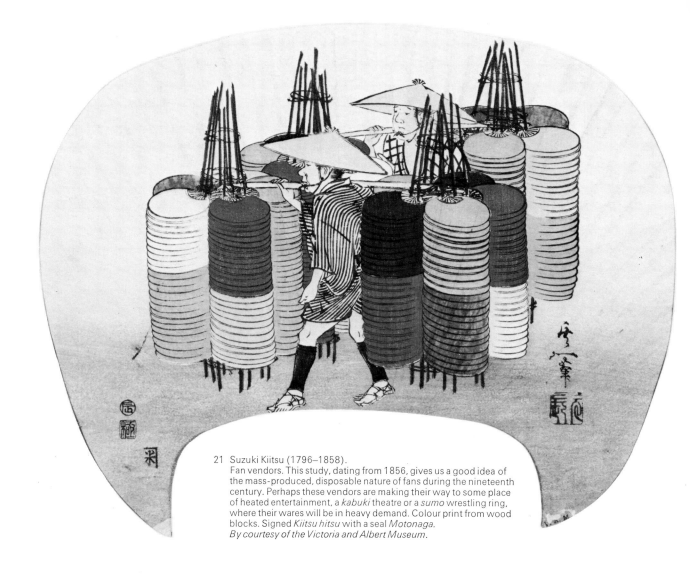

21 Suzuki Kiitsu (1796–1858).
    Fan vendors. This study, dating from 1856, gives us a good idea of
    the mass-produced, disposable nature of fans during the nineteenth
    century. Perhaps these vendors are making their way to some place
    of heated entertainment, a *kabuki* theatre or a *sumo* wrestling ring,
    where their wares will be in heavy demand. Colour print from wood
    blocks. Signed *Kiitsu hitsu* with a seal *Motonaga*.
    By courtesy of the Victoria and Albert Museum.

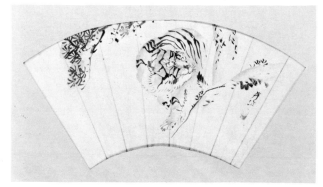

22 Kishi Gantai (1782–1865).
    Tiger prowling beneath a pine tree. Although the tiger was a
    favourite subject with Ganku, father of Gantai and founder of the
    Kishi school, Gantai does not slavishly follow his father's manner
    here. Instead of the detailed surface textures typical of the father in
    his tiger paintings we have an impressionistic account which owes
    more to the Shijo style. Ink on paper. Signed *Gantai* with two seals.
    By courtesy of Dennis Wiseman.

23 Fan-shaped plate with a floral design in overglaze enamels. The
    fan shape was frequently used for ceramic objects but it is unusual
    to find a plate like this one, which is rendered almost entirely useless
    by the folds. It was probably intended for decorative use only.
    Kyoto ware, eighteenth or nineteenth century.
    By courtesy of the Victoria and Albert Museum.

24 Utagawa Kuniyoshi (1797–1861).
Design for a fan print: the actor Sawamura Sojuro. Print artists were responsible for the design and not the execution of their works. The artist's (or his assistant's) final drawing for a print was usually destroyed in the process of block-cutting and this example is more in the nature of a preliminary sketch. Ink on paper. Circa 1835.
By courtesy of the Victoria and Albert Museum.

25 Fukutomi Tansui (dates unknown).
A scene in Yokohama. After the imperial restoration of 1868 Japan embarked upon a period of massive industrial and commercial expansion in which Yokohama, the port of Tokyo, played an important part. At the same time Western techniques of print making from metal plates were reintroduced, as in this example. The flags of Japan, Britain and the United States can be seen. Signed *drawn with the iron brush by Fukutomi Tansui*. Circa 1880.
By courtesy of Martin Willcocks.

26 Okada Beisanjin (1744–1820).
Grape vine and a Buddha's hand citrus. Ink on paper. Signed *painted by Beisanjin at the age of seventy three* with a seal *Denkoku no in*.
By courtesy of Dennis Wiseman.

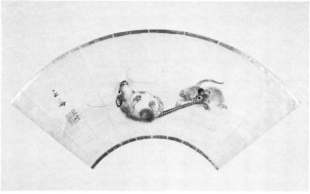

28 Satake Eikai (1803–1874).
Rats and eggs. Rats, which are associated in the popular mind
with Daikoku, the god of wealth, have not usually been looked on
in Japan with the displeasure accorded to them in the West.
Ink and colours on paper, with touches of gold.
Signed *Eikai* with a seal *Satake no in*.
Reproduced by courtesy of the Trustees of the British Museum.

27 Probably by Hiroshige II (1826–1869).
The bay at Kuroto in Kazusa province, from a series of views of the
provinces. This print, probably by Hiroshige's pupil and adopted
son, is unusual in retaining its original mount, consisting of a piece
of bamboo split at one end into more than fifty splints which pass
between the papers of the fan and are held in place by a thin
frame. Signed *Hiroshige ga*. ? 1858.
By courtesy of the Gulbenkian Museum of Oriental Art, Durham.

29 Matsuya Jichosai (fl. 1781–1788).
The seven gods of good fortune. Jichosai, a *sake* brewer, writer,
and painter who lived in Osaka, was famous for his sketchy,
cartoon-like style. The seven gods may be partially identified as
follows (reading from right to left) : Daikoku holding a mallet,
Ebisu with a fishing rod and a fish, Jurojin with his deer, Fukurokuju
with his high forehead. Hotei accompanied by a Chinese boy and
Benten, the only female among the seven. It is not easy to associate
the seventh god, Bishamon, with either of the two figures at right
and left. Ink on paper. Signed *Jichosai* with two seals.
By courtesy of Dennis Wiseman.

30 *Suehiro ogi* ('wide-ended fan').
This type of fan, which takes its name from its appearance when
closed, became popular during the fifteenth century and is
particularly associated with the *No* drama and the Buddhist
priesthood.
Nineteenth century.
By courtesy of the Victoria and Albert Museum.

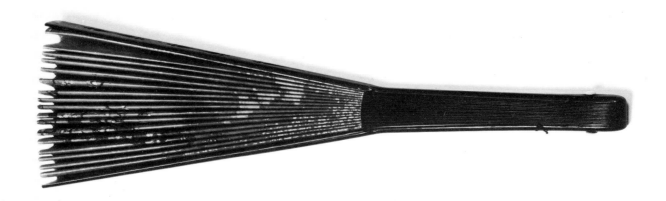

The renewed contact with China mentioned above in connection with the Muromachi period had a profound influence on Japanese culture in general and on painting in particular and it was not long before monochrome paintings in the Chinese manner were being produced by Japanese artists, who rapidly created their own distinct style. Our evidence for fan painting in the hundred and fifty years from the end of the fifteenth century is considerably enriched by the curious practice current at that time of fixing large numbers of painted fans to folding screens or, on occasion, painting fan shapes directly onto screens. For the reasons given above we can no longer pin down a clearly definable range of subject matter, nor would it be appropriate here to embark on a history of Japanese painting; but as far as composition is concerned we may note that by comparison with the *Lotus Sutra* leaves, the placing of individual elements is no longer dominated to such an extent by the radii of the fan, although the curved horizon is still in widespread use.

The late sixteenth and the seventeenth century saw a resurgence of the native painting tradition in which decorative effect was a prime consideration and this movement sees its culmination in the work of Tawaraya Sotatsu (died circa 1642), who was born into a fan-making family and continued to paint fans throughout his life. Compositional methods appropriate to the fan shape are evident in Sotatsu's work whatever its format: radiation from a rivet, real or imaginary; placing of pictorial elements in a series of arcs; and (although this derives ultimately from the narrative scrolls) progression from right to left. Sotatsu was also conscious of another problem of fan painting which had been largely ignored by his predecessors: even when open the fan is still slightly folded. To counteract the distortion resulting from this he prolongs the horizontals in his compositions. When his fan paintings are flattened and mounted as we usually see them today, they do not reflect his original intentions. The decorative tradition in Edo painting was carried on by Ogata Korin (1658–1716), another artist with a penchant for fan-painting, both in the *uchiwa* and the folding fan format, and was revived again by Sakai Hoitsu (1761–1828) (plate 6).

The *ukiyoe* school has already been mentioned for the evidence it affords us on the widespread use of fans during the Tokugawa period; in addition the *ukiyoe* print, which could be produced in large numbers, was extremely suitable for the decoration of fans. Hiroshige (1797–1858), well known for his landscape prints, was prolific in this field and like most *ukiyoe* fan-designers he usually confined himself to screen fans, almost always producing them in the characteristic shapes seen, for example, in plate 9 and fig. 16. The upright folding fan shape was also popular, especially for portraits (plate 10).

The governmental system brought in by Tokugawa Ieyasu took as its ideological basis the social and moral concepts of Confucianism and the introduction of this Chinese philosophy (which had before this time never been as influential in Japan as Buddhism) was the cause of a new wave of interest in things Chinese. Although the Tokugawa period is generally thought of as a time of total isolation, Chinese and Dutch merchants were in fact still allowed to reside at the port of Nagasaki, and it was through the medium of the Chinese merchants that two important manuals on Chinese painting were introduced to Japan during the seventeenth century, the *Pa-chung Hua-p'u* ('Album of eight types of painting', *Hasshu Gafu* in Japanese, first printed in Japan in 1671) and the *Chieh-tzu-yuan Hua-chuan* ('Painting tradition of the mustard seed garden', *Kaishien Gaden* in Japanese, not printed in Japan until 1748, but widely known long before that date). Both books contain sections devoted to the fan shape and it is interesting to note that Ike no Taiga (1723–1776), one of the best known artists of the Chinese-inspired school known as *Nanga*, is said to have collaborated with his mother in his youth in the running of a fan shop at which he sold fans adorned with paintings taken from the *Hasshu Gafu*. Fan painting, in fact, was an important part of the output of most *Nanga* artists. Their classic Chinese-type landscapes often follow the composition of the fan paintings in the Chinese manuals and almost wilfully ignore the fan shape; with other subjects, however, they take full advantage of the difficulties (or opportunities) offered by the format. This contrast is well illustrated in two paintings by Tani Buncho reproduced here (figs. 17 and 18).

In the second half of the eighteenth century two related schools of painting, the Maruyama and the Shijo, came into prominence. It is difficult to sum up their distinguishing characteristics in a few words but they may be said to have attempted to combine traditional techniques of brushwork with a close observation of nature; the result is not a slavish realism but a vividly transmitted response to the essence of things which is well illustrated in the three fans by Chinnen, Hogyoku and Gantai (fig. 19, plate 20 and fig. 22).

Notes

1 Nakamura Kiyoe, *Ogi to Ogie* ('Fans and Fan Painting'), Kyoto, Kawara Shoten, 1969, pp. 9–12.
2 The *Wamyoruijusho* of Minamoto no Shitagau. See Minamoto, T., in Nakamura Kiyoe and others, *Nihon no Mon'yo: Ogi* ('Japanese Motifs: The Fan'), Kyoto, Korinsha, 1971, p. 12.
3 The same characters are used as in modern Japanese. See Noma Seiroku, *Soshingu* ('Personal Decoration'), *Nihon no Bijutsu* no. 1, Tokyo, Shibundo, 1966.
4 The *T'u-hua chien-wen chih* of Kuo Jo-hsü. See Minamoto, T., loc. cit., p. 12.
5 Ivan Morris (trans. and ed.), *The Pillow Book of Sei Shonagon*, London, Oxford University Press, 1967, section 263.
6 Ibid., section 37.
7 The fans shown in the *Choju Giga* ('Animal Caricatures') have fewer sticks, but this is probably due to the sketchy style of the painting.
8 Illustrated in Nakamura Kiyoe, *Nihon no Ogi* ('Fans of Japan'), Kyoto, Oyashima Shuppan, 1942, 1946, plate facing p. 123.
9 For example the *Makura no Soshi Emaki*.
10 In the Okura Shukokan. A similar example of later date is in Tokyo National Museum.

L'AIR.

AER.

C. Prind. S. Cæs. M.   Gox Senior delin. et exend. Iunior Sculp.

31
'L'Air'.
Engraving from
the set "Les
Elements" by
Jean-Baptiste
Pillement,
circa 1767.

Chapter 3 Chinoiserie

The Fan Circle and the Victoria and Albert Museum

Chinoiserie is the French term adopted in the nineteenth century to describe the European fashion for articles in the Chinese taste. It was at its height from the late seventeenth to the third quarter of the eighteenth century, and within the decorative arts tended to include as inspiration any article made east of what was then Constantinople.

Goods from the East have been rare and highly prized since Roman times. The caravans from Central Asia continued to bring silks, spices, and other precious and sought-after objects for sale in Europe throughout the Middle Ages. The travels of Marco Polo, known through many editions from the late fourteenth century, had both clarified and obscured the characteristics of the far 'Land of Cathay' and the court of Kublai Khan. With the weakening of the vast Mongol Empire, which extended over almost the whole of Central Asia, and the consequent disruption of the overland routes, trade with Europe diminished, though there was sporadic maritime contact which increased with the European penetration of the 'Eastern Seas'.

Vasco da Gama's success in finding a sea route to India in 1498 paved the way for increased commerce. The pioneers of trade with the orient were the Portuguese, who by 1511 controlled the Banda States, the West Coast of India and the entrance to the Persian Gulf. In Molucca they set up an entrepôt for goods from all over the East and by 1544 they were in contact with Japan. Their defeat by the Spaniards in 1543 laid the area open to the other Western European nations who organised companies to exploit and develop the trade. The English founded the East India Company in 1600, closely followed by the Dutch Vereenigde Ost-Indische Compagnie in 1602, while the French Compagnie des Indes was not consolidated until 1664 under the aegis of Colbert[1].

The records show the enormous quantity of goods imported: tea, textiles, porcelain, lacquer work, and among other items, both fans and fan sticks (plate 14). The Minutes of the East India Company[2], dated 1st October 1614, mention 'paper fannes' together with 'China dishes and the like' as commodities suitable for sale in Britain and by 1699, according to the East India Company Letter Book[3], '20,000 fans of the finest and richest lacquer sticks' could be bought at Canton and Amoy. Sheer quantity would seem to have swamped the market, and by 1700 it is suggested that 'the town is so stocked with the ordinary and middling fans they will not turn to account[4]', and that only 'fine new fashioned, the sticks the finest and richest lacquered . . . and several of them ivory' would find purchasers. The types imported at this period in such large quantities are discussed in the article on Chinese fans, but very few seem to have survived, though there still exist several examples of ivory and lacquered sticks.

By the middle of the eighteenth century English fan-makers were becoming seriously concerned with the competition from the Far East. They had tried direct imitation and according to Savary de Bruslons, they were most skilled, better indeed than the French at making copies of the much prized imports from China. Under the heading 'Eventail' in his Dictionnaire Universel de Commerce[5], 1723, he states *'les Eventails de la Chine & ceux d'Angleterre qui les imitent si parfaitement, sont les plus en Vogue; & il faut avouer que les uns ont un si beau lacque, & que les autres sont si bien montez, que quoiqu'en tout le reste ils cédent aux beaux Eventails de France, ils leur sont au moins préférables par ces deux qualitez'*. It is unfortunate that we do not know to which sort of fan he refers.

The main pressure appears to have built up at the lower end of the market. The English fan makers' complaint of 1752 to the East India Company, as reported in Felix Farley's Bristol Journal[6], deals with the grievance of 'a great Number of Poor Fanstick Makers, and others, occupying different Branches of the Fan Trade' and sets out 'the Hardships they labour under by the Importation of India fans'. At the same time reports appear in the Daily Advertiser and were picked up by the Gentleman's Magazine[7]. It was a popular or at least a well publicized campaign. If it is the same grievance that is dealt with in the undated broadside 'The Fan Makers Grievance by the Importation of Fans from the East Indies'[8], their next ploy was to attempt to convince Parliament of their plight; imploring the House of Commons to restrict imports of fans and fansticks, suggested to have recently numbered 550,000, which injured the livelihood of 'Hundreds of Poor Artificers concerned with the Sticks, Papers, Leathers, in ordering the Silk . . . likewise . . . imployed in Painting, Varnishing and Japanning'. In the following year, February 1753, they turned from pathos to persuasion, presenting the Princess Dowager of Wales with 'a Fan superior to Indian fans' which she was 'graciously pleased to accept'[9]. She did not lack grounds for comparison for in her household accounts for 1732/3 there is a bill which mentions 'Indian Read stick fans', presumably of red Chinese lacquer and in 1732/3 '7.7.0' was expended with J. de Colima on 'Seven fine India fans'[10].

There were encouraging precedents for an appeal for Government intervention and protection against goods from the East Indies. The weavers had succeeded in getting Indian silks and printed calicos entirely banned in 1700, and the joiners and japanners had persuaded Parliament to raise the tax on imported lacquer-work in 1702[11]. The fan-makers were less successful. Their appeal was heard by the court of the East India Company – and sent back to them[12]. No action was taken. If there was a complaint to the House of Commons it is not noted in the journals. The taxes on fans remained almost unchanged throughout the period and it is explicitly stated in the preamble to the 1724 Book of Rates[13], which put a duty on Calpins or fan leaves, that the act does not apply to goods from the East Indies, which were separately rated. But by 1738 there does appear to have been an attempt to restrict imports, not by imposing a new act but by reactivating an old one, 3 Edward IV, which forbids the

32 Fan painted in gouache, *Chinoiserie* design with inlaid ivory
sticks. German, circa 1760. The design recalls Blanc de Chine
figures and the work of Pillement.
*By courtesy of the Osterreichisches Museum für Angewandte
Kunst (Figder Collection), Vienna.*

33 Fan, black and white pen drawing on kid showing a *Chinoiserie*
landscape which includes a motif derived from the Pillement
design 'l'air'. The sticks are of carved and pierced mother-of-pearl
inlaid with silver gilt foil. French, circa 1760.
From the Messel Collection: by courtesy of the Countess of Rosse.

34 Fan of paper with printed design of *Chinoiserie* scene flanked by
European landscapes. Painted ivory sticks and plain ivory guard.

Marked and dated S. Clark, 1744.
By courtesy of George Borchard.

importation of many accessories and luxuries made abroad.
It was not enough. Fans, small and light, were an obvious
temptation to smugglers. Evasion was possible and one of
the grievances of 1752 was that 'India fans, the chief Part of
which being run ashore, pay neither Duty nor Indulgence',
and the smuggled goods were sold at a mere 6d each[8]. The
crowning insult was that these injurious imports were copies,
for according to the fan-makers, 'Our Patterns and Models
are carried over for the Indians to work by'.

With both Chinese and English workmen striving to copy
one another, identification presents problems which are by
no means solved yet. The situation is further complicated by
the fact that fans are made from different components and
diverse materials, each of which may have a separate origin.
Moreover, a systematic reconsideration of European fan
collections is only just beginning, and the characteristics of
the '*Chinoiserie*' as opposed to the Chinese fan are only now
being evaluated.

It requires an experienced eye to tell Chinese from
European painting and keen sight to distinguish the splutter
of the European quill from the tapering line of a Chinese
brush stroke. All that is common is design in the Chinese
taste and this can incorporate elements from China, Japan,
India and Persia, transmuted by occidental hands and eyes,
and with a history going back at least to the seventeenth
century.

The earliest practitioner seems to have been Mathias
Beitler whose designs in this style are dated 1616. As
decorated objects from the East came to Europe in greater
quantities and illustrated accounts of travels to China
proliferated, many sets of engravings appeared, catering for
an increased popular appreciation of the exotic. In the
Treatise on Japanning and Varnishing by John Stalker and
George Parker (1688) a well-known English practical
application of this style, buildings of bizarre proportions,
exotic birds and oriental figures, almost as 'Persian' as
they are Chinese, are illustrated. There are numerous other
examples in Holland and Germany but the engravings
Picturae Sinicae, 1702 (see 11), produced by Peter Schenk
Sr (1660 to 1718 or 1719) of Amsterdam would, together with

35 Fan, stamped paper leaf printed with a *Chinoiserie* scene hand coloured in watercolours. The initials FM and date 1763 in script but reversed. The sticks are bone. English, 1763. *By courtesy of George Borchard.*

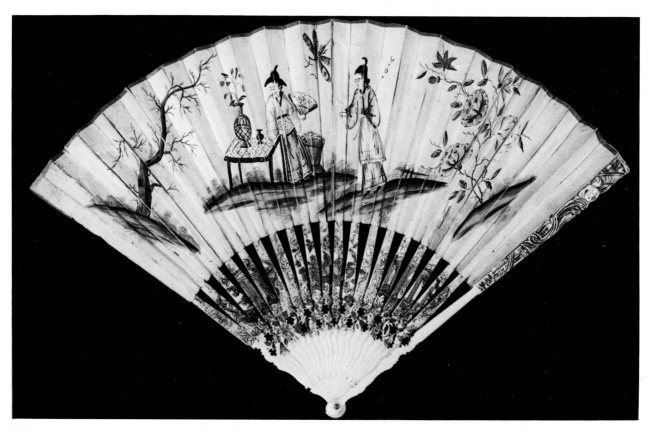

36 Fan of paper painted in gouache with a *Chinoiserie* design and having sticks and guard of carved and painted ivory. Probably French, circa 1760. *By courtesy of the Musée Carnavalet, Paris.*

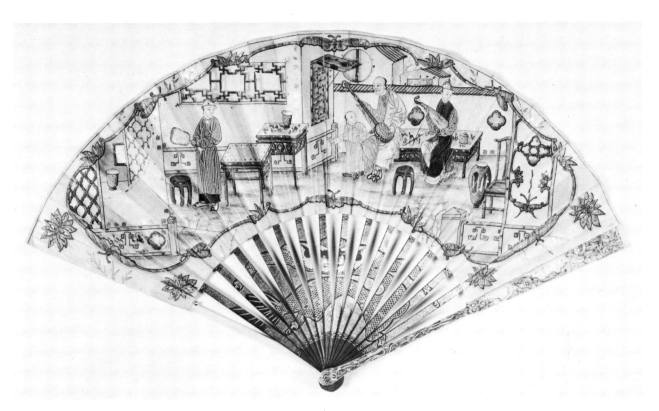

37 Fan with paper leaf on which a Chinese terrace is depicted in watercolour with mica insertions. On the reverse is another view of the
terrace in the same technique. The sticks are lacquer and the guard
ivory with mother-of-pearl inlay. This fan is Chinese made for the
export market and may be compared with a similar example (plate 15)
possibly not Chinese.
By courtesy of the Victoria and Albert Museum.

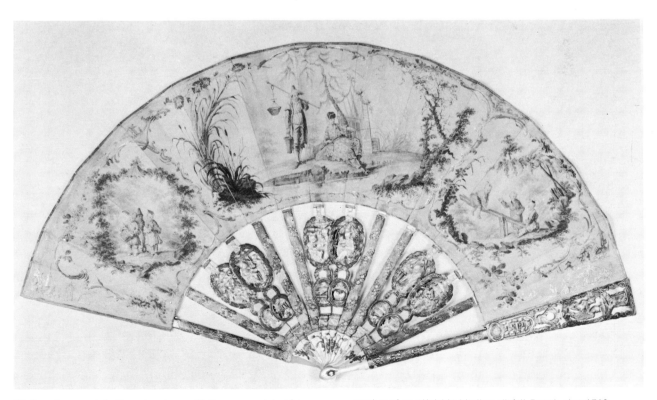

38 Fan of paper painted in watercolours with three scenes taken from
the works of Jean Pillement. The sticks and guard are of carved
mother-of-pearl inlaid with silver gilt foil. French, circa 1760.
By courtesy of the Victoria and Albert Museum.

Stalker and Parker, seem to give a distinct bearing on the designs of a series within a group of painted and varnished ivory brisé fans, of about 1710 to 20, which older writers often refer to as '*Vernis Martin*'. The series is large, suggesting that the fans were as prized in their own day as they were to be in the mid-nineteenth century, and the popularity of the type as *objects de luxe* and collectors' items, has led to a great deal of overpainting and possibly to the making of misleading reproductions. They have travelled widely and original attributions are lost. On grounds of style they have been associated with France, Holland, and Germany, but what they all have in common is a main motif on the leaf, biblical, classical or European genre, perhaps scenes from Racine's plays[14], flanked by *Chinoiserie* vignettes and Chinese style figures painted on the gorge.

The Court of Louis XIV loved objects in the Chinese taste and were ably served by Jean Bérain (1640–1711). He designed Chinese masque costumes and the '*Collation à la Chinoise*' he designed for the King's brother, Monsieur, was systematically Chinese in inspiration. But, as far as the fans are concerned, his main contribution was that offshoot of his grotesques, the Singerie, in which monkeys replace classical fauns. This idea was later followed by Antoine Watteau (1684–1721) who invented charming creations, monkeys which were behaving like true Parisians. A fan from the Schreiber collection in the British Museum of the mid-eighteenth century is a good example of the type, though it includes other animals besides monkeys.

Chinoiserie and Rococo are blended by Watteau and Francois Boucher (1703–1770) and motifs similar to Boucher's Fishing Party and his tapestry designs, 1742, the *Tenture Chinoise*, can be seen on several fans. There have been many attempts to credit these artists with specific fans, but none have been successful.

Jean-Baptiste Pillement (1719–1808), the artist and engraver, published sets of designs with motifs deriving from these and other artists. A high proportion of them are '*à la Chinoise*'. They were widely used for a number of decorative purposes and the leaf of a fine fan from the Messel collection (fig. 33) dating from about 1770, incorporates his motif '*l'air*', from the set '*Les Elements*', published in 1767. A much used compilation of examples of his and others' work, which includes Chinese and other fashionable and contemporary motifs, is the 'Ladies Amusement', 1760, and many of the engravings are similar to those found on fans.

This, and other pattern books, such as those of Sir William Chambers (1726–1796), 'Designs of Chinese Buildings and Furniture' (1757) and William Halfpenny's 'Chinese and Gothic Architecture properly ornamented' (1750), provide a large repertoire on which the fan-makers drew to provide something which the public would find more to its taste than the actual products of China.

Sticks as well as leaves are affected. Chinese figures are sometimes painted or carved on guards and there are even imitations of oriental lacquer work, though black and red sticks are usually of Chinese origin. A distinctive type of stick of about 1760, which when closed resembles a bundle of rods, has been termed 'Pagoda'[15]. It is not easy to justify this from eighteenth century design sources. The gorge,

when open, has a certain angularity of pattern which is often associated with Chinese motifs, but the rods are not treated like bamboo and if they could be said to resemble anything are most like the legs of the Gothic chair designed by Charles Manwaring in 1760[16]. They could also be said to look like a conventionalized set of classical *fasces*, but whether in refined or degenerate form they are not at all like the Chinese furniture illustrated by Sir William Chambers in 1757.

The English fan-makers must have been successful in capturing the home market, for the number of fans in the Chinese taste but not of oriental workmanship outnumber the surviving imports from China during the eighteenth century. One resource for the European craftsman facing competition from the East, was to copy a type within the Chinese repertoire. There is a large and widely distributed series dating from the middle of the eighteenth century which has highly-coloured *Chinoiserie* scenes on the leaf, carried out with an elaborate and time-consuming craftsmanship and characterised by the use of applied decoration, feathers, straw, mica and even butterfly wings, these last identified as being of West European origin[17]. In addition, they are usually painted in gouache on a ground of vellum, paper or silk. Metallic lustre paper was sometimes used to enhance the effect. Their Chinese origin is discussed in Chapter I, their European source is as yet uncertain possibly they are Dutch. Any aesthetic debt they owed to the East they paid by providing models for the Chinese 'hundred faces' applied fans of the late eighteenth and early nineteenth century, dealt with in the article on Chinese fans.

An alternative was to undercut the cheap Chinese product by mass-production. The eighteenth century saw an enormous rise in the number of engraved fans, known possibly from the sixteenth, and certainly from the early seventeenth century. In England this had great repercussions on the craft. In 1741, the House of Commons Journal[18] records a petition of the fan-painters 'representing the inconvenience of suffering them to be printed', and pointing out that within the previous three years the increase in copper plate engraving had been putting the fan-painter out of business: 'One engraver and two painters can make more in one month than the kingdom can use in a year'. As a result the export market for the well-painted fan was being lost. However, a new one was being gained and that discriminating lady Madame de Pompadour asked her brother in 1760 to provide her with printed English fans for presents, not so pretty perhaps but certainly cheaper than could be obtained elsewhere[19]. A very high proportion of the fans in the *Chinoiserie* mode are printed.

The provisions of the Engraving Copyright Act, 1734, ensure that all British engravings, fans included, are marked with their date, and the name of the artist or engraver. If on the border, too close a trim can remove the inscription, but fortunately some fans are marked on the leaf itself. Such precise dating is a great help in establishing a chronology, but differences of date are not reflected in any change or development of motif. A fan by S. Clark, signed and dated 1744, (fig. 34) and another with the initials F.M., dated 1763 (fig. 35) show little change or development in style.

39/40 Fan with paper leaf engraved and hand coloured with a
design of the five senses as ladies in fashionable dress and a
Chinoiserie design on the reverse. Marked 'BLD' 1230. French,
circa 1830.
By courtesy of the Musée Carnavalet, Paris.

41 Fan with fine kid leaf painted in gouache with *Chinoiserie* design on the reverse. Carved mother-of-pearl sticks and guard.

French, circa 1800.
By courtesy of the Musée Carnavalet, Paris.

42 Fan with paper leaf printed and hand-stained with a Japanese motif and overprinted with 'GM LOUVRE'. Wooden sticks and guard. This fan was probably commissioned in Japan and intended to publicize the Paris shop 'Les Grands Magasins du Louvre'. French, circa 1900.
By courtesy of the Musée Carnavalet, Paris.

43 Fan of ivory painted and varnished with a scene of the apotheosis from Iphigènie by Racine. The gorge is decorated with *Chinoiserie* motifs. Possibly Dutch, 1710–20.
By courtesy of the Victoria and Albert Museum.

The mixture of motif tends to be eclectic. The S. Clark fan has the design of a Chinese lady under a parasol, but she is flanked by small Italianate townscapes, one inhabited by people in the dress of the 1740s, while the other shows a figure in classical drapery. Another fan, also signed by S. Clark and dated 1740, from the Schreiber collection, shows Greenwich Park and the Thames, with a *Chinoiserie* design on either side[20].

Sometimes, mid-eighteenth century fans in the Chinese style are additionally decorated with what we call *découpage*, patterns of holes made with pins or knives. In the eighteenth century this technique would have been called *pîqure* which Diderot, in his '*Encyclopèdie des Sciences*' (1751–1765)[21] defines as '*ornements que l'on fait sur une étoffe par compartiment et avec symétrie, en la piquant et coupant avec un emporte-pièce de fer tranchant*'. The technique[22] is particularly valid in this context because cut paper work was as characteristic of Japan and China as it was popular in Europe during the eighteenth and nineteenth century. The more geometric examples are reminiscent of the earliest folding fans known in Europe dating from the mid-sixteenth century[15] which have decorations '*à jour*' in imitation of the *reticella*[23] lace of Italy. Others recall nothing so much as a twentieth-century cake doily. There is a printed fan of 1763 (fig. 35) which has a design rather like the fret ornament of houses in the Chinese style to be found in the work of Sir William Chambers, but blended with a scrolling Indian type leaf. It is probable that a template was used for the stamping. The designs repeat and are so organised as to cover the greatest amount of ground with the least effort. They are pierced or stamped through the unmounted but painted fan leaf, already lined, bound and folded into convenient segments. Considerable care is taken to avoid the picture. The use of lustre paper, heavier in quality, gives additional durability and adds to the effect.

By the end of the eighteenth century Chinese figures have begun to change and become softer and less rigidly posed, with more expressive faces. Those on a fan of circa 1800, the guards of which bear Jasper-ware medallions, flanking a central applied mezzotint by Angelica Kauffmann are reminiscent of figures in the decorations of the Brighton Pavilion (plate 16).

The popular preference was now for the classical motif, and *Chinoiserie* suffered a recession, though it never entirely disappeared. There was a revival in the 1830s, and the printed fan (figs. 39 and 40), has a Chinese motif on the reverse of a very fashionably dressed set of the five senses.

After the opening of Japan to European trade in 1854, the distinctive contribution of Japan began to supplant that of China, though at first only at the highest aesthetic level. Prints were imported in great numbers and greatly influenced artists such as Manet, Degas, Toulouse-Lautrec and Whistler. A new concept of pattern and the use of space merged imperceptibly with the *art nouveau* movement. The most fashionable fan artist in this style was Ernest Kees[24]. By the 1880s, largely due to the efforts of Arthur Lasenby Liberty (1843 to 1917)[25] and his Eastern Bazaar, Japanese fans and other artifacts were among the furnishings of almost

44 Interior of the Chinese Drawing Room at Schloss Hetzendorf,
Vienna, showing the rosewood and lacquered and gilded
panelling and the carved soap-stone fan motifs. Designed by the
Court architect Count Nikolaus von Paccassi for the use of the
widowed Empress Elizabeth, 1742–1745. The fans are modelled
on Chinese and Japanese ones of the date.
By courtesy of the Austrian Cultural Institute.

every 'artistic' English home, and sunflowers and other characteristic decorative devices had seeped into the repertoire. One painting by Manet, *La Japonaise*, 1864, (frontispiece), shows the charm of the fashion, the caricatures of the artistically pretentious by George du Maurier, another aspect. The brightly-coloured calico fan, circa 1880 (plate 19), summarises the decorative motifs, but on far too many, especially amateur work so popular at the time, there is simply a concentration of sunflowers, and a tendency to make the guards look like bamboo. Fans by Degas, with their asymmetric motifs and dramatic use of space, are hardly ever to be seen in public collections.

Any attempt by Europeans to adopt the Japanese style in its natural form and at a commercial level would undoubtedly have been swamped by the immediate availability of an enormous quantity of genuine Japanese artifacts.

Notes

1 The whole subject of Eastern trade and its influences is treated in: H. Honour, Chinoiserie: The Vision of Cathay, London 1961, O. Impey, Chinoiserie: The Impact of Oriental Styles on Western Art and Decoration, London, 1977, M. Jourdain and R. Soame Jenyns, Chinese Export Art in the Eighteenth Century London, 1950.
2 India Office Archives, East India Company Minutes, 1st October 1614.
3 India Office Archives, East India Company Letter Book X f 207 ff.
4 India Office Archives, East India Company Letter Book X f 357/8.
5 J. Savary de Bruslons Dictionnaire Universel de Commerce, 17 23, Vol I A–E, p. 1178–9.
6 London. The Fan Circle, Newsletter 4, Spring, 1977, p. 8, the entire extract relating to the Fan-makers' petition from Lisa Clinton quoting from Felix Farley's Bristol Journal, Saturday, October 28th to Saturday, November 4th, 1752.
7 Gentleman's Magazine, 2nd November, 1752, Vol. XXII, p. 533.
8 (BL) 816 M 12 (97).
9 Gentleman's Magazine, Vol. XXIII, p. 97.
10 Windsor, Royal Archives.
11 Hans Huth, Lacquer of the West, Chicago, 1971. This deals with the effect of oriental crafts on the West and European design sources for 17th and 18th century lacquer are very fully treated on pp. 27–8. The designs by Peter Schenk are illustrated in Chisaburo Yamada, Die Chinamode des Spätbarock, Berlin, 1934.
12 India Office Library, East India Company, Court Minutes 25.X.1752.
13 II George I Cap 7.
   The duties paid on imported fans are most succintly set out in Mac Iver Percival, The Fan Book, London, 1920, p. 261 which quotes the Observations of the Importation of French or Foreign Fans which appear in the 1775 volume of the Minute Book of the Worshipful Company of Fan makers; 'Calpins for Fans (Mounts). By the 11th George the First Chapter the Seventh Calpins for Fans are rated in the Custom House Books for Seven Shillings and sixpence a Dozen the Duty paid on Importation is one shilling five pence seven eighths per dozen. And besides if made of leather and the leather be the most valuable part. For every twenty shillings of the real value upon cash the Duty upon importation is six shillings.
   By the 12th of Charles the 2nd Chapter the fourth Fans for women and children (French making) are rated in the Custom House Book at £2 per dozen and the Duty paid on importation £1-5-0 per dozen.
   BUT if the Fans are painted they are prohibited to be imported and are seizable as *painted wares*. It then proceeds to retail the provisions of 3 Edward IV modified by 6th Anne 19, which extends the embargo to items of which prohibited articles form part 'Upon which Act it appears that either Mounts or Fans that are painted are seizable and that Fans or Mounts Embellished with Gold or Silver are Prohibited under very severe penalties'. It comments on the Commercial Treaty with France, 10th May 1787, and concludes that 'Paper Fan Mounts plain cannot be imported without paying a Duty of £55 per cent. And that Plain Fans cannot be imported without paying a Duty of £27-10 per cent or £33 if imported as toys.' The memorandum accords with facts from other sources such as H. Crouch, A Complete View of the British Customs, of which there are several editions, 1724, 1725, 1732, 1738 and 1746 and each is amended. It is the third edition, 1738, which notes the reactivation and application of 3 Edward IV. S. Baldwin, A Survey of the British Customs 1770 includes all laws up to the end of the Session 9 George III.
14 London, Victoria & Albert Museum, T78. 1956 shows a scene from *Iphigénie* and there is another in a private collection with a scene from Andromaque.
15 G. Wooliscroft Rhead, History of the Fan, opp. p. 118, shows a fan with a Pagoda stick. T382-1950 (Victoria and Albert Museum) is a rather fine quality example. Plate 72 shows a decoupé seventeenth century fan.
16 Charles Manwering, Designs for Furniture, 1760, Plate 172.
17 The Wings of Lysandra Bellargus have been identified on a mid-eighteenth century fan in a French Collection.
18 House of Commons Journal, Vol. XXIII, p. 606 (53).
19 Nancy Mitford, Madame de Pompadour Rev. Ed. 1968, p. 232.
20 London, British Museum, Department of Prints and Drawings, Lionel Cust, Catalogue of the Fans and Fan leaves in the Schreiber Collection, 1901.
21 C. Diderot, Encyclopèdie ou Dictionnaire Raisonné des Sciences . . . 25 Vols, Neuchâtel 1751–65. Ref. Piqure. Decouper is defined as the process of stamping out button blanks artificial flower leaves and making pinked decorations on garments.
22 A. Tuer, Old Fashioned Children's Books, 1864. The Book of delightful and strange designs . . . The Art of the Japanese Stencil Cutter.
23 Stamped lace-like patterns can be found on other cheap accessories in the eighteenth Century such as aprons and ladies' hats. It is possible that this process also has a Chinese origin, for Savary (op. cit.), p. 1178–9, refers to a fabric CHA, a light silk which the Chinese wore in summer, some of which is 'percées a jour & uividees comme les dentelles d'Angleterre & quelque fois en si grande quantité qu'on ne voit pas le corps de l'etoffe'.
24 Les Modes, 1907, p. 14.
25 Alison Adburgham. Liberty's: a Biography of a Shop, London, 1975.

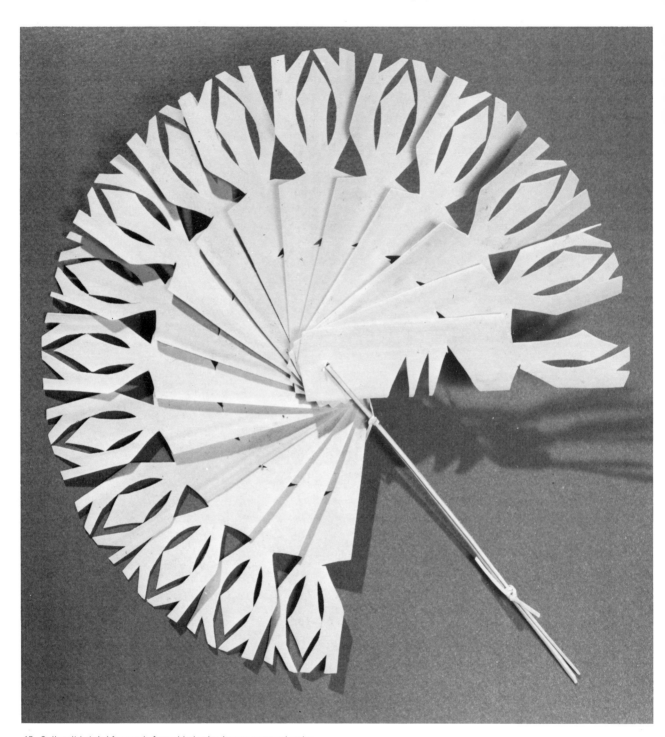

45 Collapsible brisé fan made from dried palm-leaves, serrated at the
edge in order for the sticks to fit together without any ribbons.
Used to decorate the Goddess Devi Sri and also for Temple
offerings, twentieth century, from South Bali.
By courtesy of Mrs N. Trevenan James.

Chapter 4 From India to the Philippines
Nancy Armstrong

The fan, like the umbrella and the fly-whisk, was regarded in the countries of the East as a solemn symbol of State. From the Seychelles to the Philippines, it may be considered as an aspect of the umbrella symbol of power, a continuous development of military and processional standards through hand-fan to fly-whisk. Its practical use must not be disregarded.

The symbolism is widespread and also occurs in European and African contexts in historic and prehistoric times, most accessibly perhaps in the ritual of the Catholic church.

As in China (see chapter 1), a man's outward appearance and possessions, especially decorative ornaments, were an expression of his wealth and stature.

Canopies and headdresses

The feathers from a rare bird, for example, worn on the head or carried as a fan, signified the social status of a ruler. In Hindi the generic term for a fan is *pankha*, from *pankh*, a feather or bird's wing. This usage is current in south-east Asia, which was strongly permeated with cultural and religious influences from the Indian sub-continent.

In many areas, the Puranic snake gods, shaded by the sacred umbrella, and attended by fan- and fly-whisk-bearers, are found, along with the sacred five- or seven-headed cobra, rearing up as a canopy for Buddha and other Hindu gods. Vishnu is sometimes represented as wearing a headdress decorated with peacock feathers, and the peacock and other stylized birds may well be connected with fan design and decoration.

Across the Pacific Ocean in New Guinea, David Attenborough's book *Zoo Quest in Paradise*[1] gives the following description of a Melanesian tribal ceremony:

We had not been walking for more than ten minutes when I heard a distant drumming and singing. We crossed one of the kunai patches and saw coming down the path towards us a spectacular procession. At its head strode several men resplendent in enormous feather headdresses and carrying long three-pronged spears. But they were merely the heralds of an even more impressive sight, for behind them came a man carrying aloft on top of a pole a giant standard, three feet across, ablaze with gorgeous colour. It was a banner of woven cane and grass hung with a dozen shining pearl shells, mats sewn with valuable cowrie shells, tiaras of scarlet parrot feathers, and around its rim thirty or forty sets of Bird of Paradise plumes . . . These men were on their way to collect a bride and this was part of the payment.

Certain sorts of ceremonial feather headdresses were common throughout the East. The Museum of Mankind owns a Talana from Assam, made from flexible strips of cane to which are attached hornbill feathers, the number signifying the owner's sexual conquests. This particular example was made by the Zemi at a training camp in the plains, but to the identical pattern used in Asulu and all Zemi villages in Assam.

A second headdress (fig. 57) is extremely dramatic, trimmed with yellow human hair, with the same sorts of shells mentioned by David Attenborough, and small red feathers. This was once owned by a Chief in Samoa. A third, (fig. 62), from New Guinea, is made of eleven cassowary quills set in a lump of beeswax with red seeds from the Fal tree and a white cockatoo feather.

Bird of Paradise plumes are also used. They live in the secluded valleys of New Guinea and there are fifty different species, the largest the size of a crow, the smallest the size of a robin, all with brilliant glossy iridescent feathers of every hue. A stuffed example is illustrated, together with a fan of Emu feathers, made by the Aborigines of Elcho Island, Northern Australia.

In the East, another bird, the peacock, with its fan-like 'hundred-eyed' tail, expresses the vigilance and magnificence of kingship. The peacock-feather emblem of royalty is the insignia of a king's office and the principal evidence of his sovereignty; in pictures and sculpture he is often accompanied by an attendant bearing this emblem. Peacock feathers can also be arranged in a panache, sometimes surrounded by egret feathers, or carried in the hand as a fixed fan.

In figure 54 a silver coffee service made in Thailand is illustrated; its decoration shows a procession of men with standard fans. The finial is shaped like a *Pertala Indera Maha Sakti*, or peacock, the thumb-piece a spreading folded fan, and the handle is composed of a sculptured snake. The silver jug has as a finial a hooded cobra and the handle is another snake.

THE UMBRELLA

The titles of the Kings of Burma included 'Lord of the twenty-four umbrellas', and the Emperors of China were always accompanied by men bearing symbolic umbrellas, even on the hunt. The link between fan and umbrella may be seen in examples from Malaysia made from a single palm leaf; figure 60 illustrates a fine small model of a state boat from Thailand used for the Kathin River ceremony, showing men with standards, oars, and umbrellas.

Nineteenth-century ceremonial umbrellas and parasols from Burma were made of painted silk, or of gilded leather (fig. 49), with finely carved handles. A folding fan from Mandalay is illustrated (fig. 59) and is said to show the last King of Burma, Thibaw Min, shaded by an umbrella, with his principal consort Supaya Lat, attended by courtiers and musicians, witnessing a play in the Royal Gardens in about 1880.

RELIGIOUS FANS

Fans were also important in religious rites, for instance those of the Jain religion, founded by Mahavira, which is based on asceticism and *ahimsa*, the theory and practice of non-violence. As a result flies and small insects were most carefully stopped from desecrating statues of the gods by

46 Double cockade fan, nineteenth or twentieth century, made in
Praslin Islands in the Seychelles, from the very rare Coco-de-Mer
palm. The seeds of this type of coconut are considered a superb
aphrodisiac, but unfortunately, these double-nut trees (thought to
have been the Fruit of Knowledge in the Garden of Eden) are
now almost extinct.
By courtesy of George Borchard

47 Crescent-shaped cotton fan embroidered with a floral design in
pink and green silk and metallic silver threads ; silver tinsel border.
The lining is probably English, Spitalfields silk 1830–40 ;
the handle of silver-gilt. This fan is said to have belonged to Warren
Hastings' second wife and was made at Murshidabad, India.
By courtesy of the Victoria and Albert Museum.

48 Fan made of woven split ivory and metallic silver thread in a
   diaper design, nineteenth century, from Sylhet in India.
   By courtesy of the Victoria and Albert Museum.

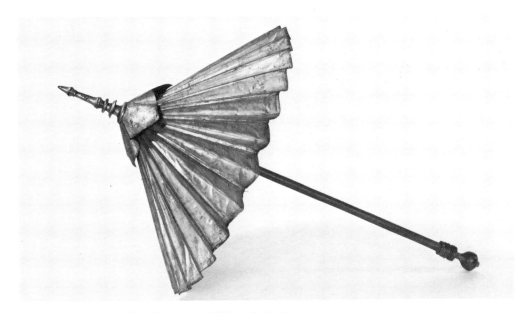

49 Very fine small parasol from Burma, circa 1886, made of vellum
   covered with gold leaf and having a turned wooden handle.
   By courtesy of George Borchard.

being brushed away with a chowrie or fly-whisk. Chowries are seen in bas-reliefs on the pagoda at Elephanta in India, and in many other places. Among the materials from which they were made are the bushy tail of the Himalayan yak, finely split sandalwood or ivory, peacock feathers, horsehair, and grasses.

One very fine chowrie, illustrated in plate 20, is an eighteenth century example, probably made in Patiala State, with very fine fronds of ivory spreading from a carved ivory cornucopia. Another type of fly-whisk, of coconut fibres set into a wooden handle, was made in Fiji, and similar ones occur in Polynesia and Melanesia, though it is difficult to say whether the fly-whisk here signified precedence or was for religious uses.

A fixed type of temple fan was made at Masulipatam in India, composed of split bamboo overlaid with papier mâché and gilt foil, and the very fine example of a brisé sandalwood temple fan came from Malaysia (fig. 51). Wafting the sandalwood fan, often first dipped in water to increase the scent and the coolness, was a delicate compliment to the gods.

In South Bali they made, and still make, models of the Goddess Devi Sri, who wore a type of fan-shaped headdress. The figurines are made from plaited vegetable fibre, the face scored on a triangular piece of leaf. They represent the Rice Goddess and are offered to the Rice Spirit after the harvest. The one in figure 53 came from Saba, South Bali. A collapsible fan, also made for Devi Sri, is illustrated in figure 45.

Shapes of fans

Shapes of fans in this area vary widely and come in five distinct types: those with handles; those where the handles are integral; brisé fans; cockade fans; and folding fans.

FANS WITH HANDLES

In India there are many fans which are crescent-shaped and have a long handle by the side, either for you to fan yourself or to be fanned by a pankha-wallah. Some of these are single and some double with an inner lining. One interesting example from Murshidabad is made from cotton embroidered in pink and green silk and metallic silver threads, and having a silver tinsel border. The long handle is of silver-gilt, but the lining material is probably eighteenth-century English Spitalfields silk (fig. 47).

There are examples of heart, flag, spade, and circular shapes, often made of reeds from southern India, and one circular fan (plate 23) is spectacular. It comes from Assam and is made from porcupine quills dyed red and white, made up with coloured straw and a fringe of peacock feathers.

FANS WITH INTEGRAL HANDLES

Apart from a few wooden fans (examples are known from Tonga, Malaysia and Sri Lanka) most fans with integral handles were made from plaited vegetable fibres such as straw, reeds, palms or fibrous grasses.

BRISÉ FANS

Brisé fans are folding ones in which the stick expands to form the leaf. They appear to have been made almost everywhere

between Sri Lanka and the Philippines.

A Sri Lanka brisé fan is illustrated (fig. 50) which is made to look like parakeets, the sticks with simple bird outlines but the guards more elaborately carved.

In Burma and Malaysia one finds temple fans of carved and pierced sandalwood; in Indonesia there are various types of brisé fans made from buffalo hide and strengthened with buffalo horn, and from the Philippines come very heavy brisé fans of speckled ebony.

COCKADE FANS

Cockade, or circular folding, fans, are also known in the East; one from Subsanghar, Assam, is a fine example of carved ivory, having a handle with panels of floral decoration terminating in an elephant's head. Both single and double cockade fans come from the Seychelles. The sticks are made from the rare double-coconut tree, the Coco-de-Mer Palm from Praslin Island. The construction of cockade fans is extremely painstaking.

FOLDING FANS

Folding fans are found all over the East; most that remain date from the nineteenth and twentieth centuries and were probably made for Europeans. There is a simple twentieth century advertising fan from Celebes, now Sulawesi, illustrated in figure 56, made from printed paper with stained bamboo sticks.

However, the most curious of all are those made from 'lace-bark'. There is an example of a section of lace-bark, *Lagetta Lintearia*, which was used unaltered, with the bark forming the handle. Another, (plate 25) made from the incredibly delicate material, is folding and has a decoration of dried and pressed ferns. The border is of Spatha, the sheath of the fruit of the Mountain Cabbage Palm, and the tassel is made from the fibre of the Pineapple Plant.

The lace-bark tree originated in the West Indies, but was introduced to Java in the nineteenth century. The 'lace' was on occasion used for clothes; there are two bonnets made from it in the Museum at Kew Botanical Gardens in London.

Colours

It has been suggested that there is an analogy between the colouring of fans and their land of origin. In the hot bare areas, from Sind to Baluchistan, through Kathiawar to Gujerat in India, parts of Malaysia, Thailand, and Indonesia, craftsmen used the deep glowing colours of velvets, tie-dyed cloths, and batiks. Further south the colours are more subdued, and in Malabar, the Seychelles, and Oceania, fans are neutrally coloured as a relief from the brilliant colours of the landscape. There are also traditional associations, among them red as a symbol of love and marriage, maroon and black for mourning, blue for Vishnu, and white for Shiva.

Patterns

Generally speaking patterns were subordinate to colour, often elementary in design, and almost abstract and linear in concept.

50 Brisé fan of sandalwood, with carved parokeets for guards and pierced parokeet shapes for the sticks ; red silk thread to join the sticks. Nineteenth century from Sri Lanka. *By courtesy of George Borchard.*

51 Processional or religious fan, brisé, carved from sandalwood, nineteenth century, from Malaysia. The handle is carved in the solid, showing two Pertala Indera Maha Sakti back to back, the twenty-five sticks are finely pierced. *From an anonymous collection.*

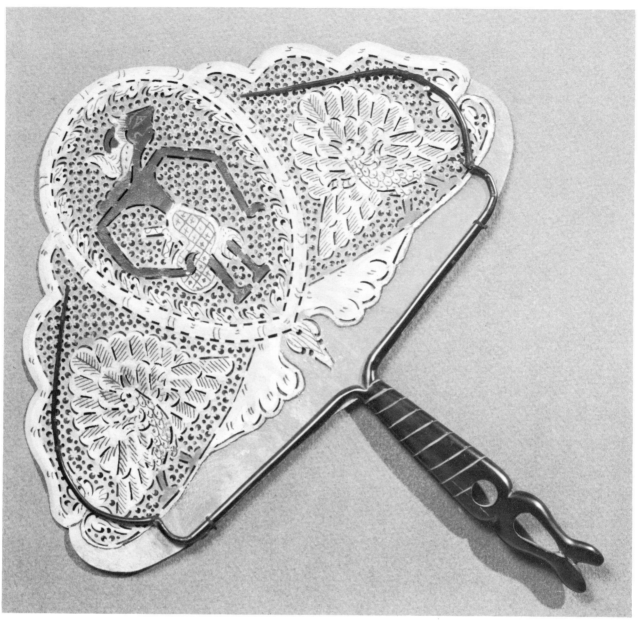

52 Fixed fan, nineteenth century, from Sumatra, made from pierced and painted buffalo hide and held by buffalo horn, decorated with the traditional Wayang shadow-puppet in a central medallion and supported by two stylized peacocks, all set within the outspread wings of a bird.
By courtesy of Martin Willcocks.

Techniques and materials

IVORY

There are references to a guild of ivory-workers in India as long ago as 200 BC, the ivory-carvers of Bhilsa at Sanchi. It is said by some that cargoes of ivory from the west of India, with the gold of Ophir, were carried in the ships of Tarshish to decorate the temple and palaces of Solomon.

Ivory has been treated in many ways: carved; veneered, as at Vizagapatam in Madras State; stained or inlaid with lac-work at Tanjore. The same technique, but in black, was practised in Mysore and at Matara in Sri Lanka. This treatment was also given to the veneered ivory of Madras State.

Ivory was finely turned in Kandy, Rajputana, Bengal, and Travancore. In the nineteenth century the most famous centres were Delhi, Amritsar, Patiala, Ambala, Ludhiana, and Lahore. In those days ivory from wild elephants was considered far superior to that of domesticated beasts, for the latter developed brittle tusks through having regular supplies of salt in their diet.

Ivory supplies came from many areas in India and Goa, Sri Lanka and Burma, and especially the Tarai in Oude, to the south-west of Nepal. Imported African ivory was also used.

53 Vegetable fibre plaited figurine, the face scored on a triangular
piece of leaf, with fan-shaped headdress trimmed in green and red.
This represents Devi Sri, the Rice Goddess, made as an offering to
the rice spirit after harvest. From Saba, between Den Pasar and
Gianyar, South Bali, nineteenth century.
*By courtesy of the Trustees of the British Museum.
Ethnography Department.*

54 Silver coffee pot and silver jug, nineteenth century, from Thailand. The design on the upper register of the coffee pot shows men with standard fans. The finial is a stylized peacock; the thumb-piece is a spread folded fan. The handle is a snake. The design on the jug is of birds and flowers; the finial is a hooded cobra and the handle is composed of a snake.
By courtesy of Mrs Erica Forbes.

The split-ivory chowrie has been mentioned – a most painstaking technique; and there are fans of woven ivory to be attached to a carved handle like a flag to a mast. These fans have lengths of silver woven into the design, and occasionally strands of the ivory stained green; several come from Sylhet. Otherwise ivory was split and made into cockade fans with ornamental handles, such as those from Subsanghar in Assam. The manufacture needed skill and patience, and was done entirely with the rudest of files, chisels, knives, etc. The main tools were a *rachi*, a *chirna*, a *roda*, and the *kharat* or turner's frame.

TEXTILE FANS

Fans in India were often made from cotton, silk, and velvet. The knowledge of silk in India came from China and there are records of the export of silk and cloth-of-gold from India to Rome in the reign of Tiberius. Of all fabrics, velvet is the one most synonymous with wealth, especially when it is treated as it is in Indian fans and covered with embroidery, gold and silver wires, and spangles.

Much Indian embroidery is of chain stitch, the centres being Kathiawar and Kach. Parts of Rajputana and the Punjab were also known for their embroidery which was distinguished by the inclusion of innumerable small discs of mirror-glass. This technique was widespread in north-west India.

Every wealthy man would have his clothes, from his fan to his shoes, embroidered with gold thread (*kalabutun*), thin tinsel (*sulma*), tinsel-wire (*mukesh*), and gold ribbon (*ghota*, *kinara*, etc.). There are examples of all these techniques illustrated (plates 26, 21 and fig. 48); a cotton fan from Murshidabad with a silver tinsel border is shown in figure 47. Red, blue, and green embroidered velvet fans incorporate wirework, gold ribbon, and spangles, called *bindli*.

The maker of spangles, the *bindligar*, used as his tools an *ahran* (small anvil), *chamra charmi* (parchment), *mikraz* (scissors), *chumti* (forceps), and *sanni* (small pincers). The *bindli* were cut out of *sitta*, thin sheets of fine gold or silver.

In Indonesia, a printed pattern is usual; tradition

55 Two fans from the Philippines, twentieth century. One is a very heavy brise fan made from speckled ebony and having a parokeet painted upon it; made for the European market and having two small mother-of-pearl engraved discs on the guards. The blue satin fan has finely carved bone sticks in the 'battoir' shape. This work is typical of the craft in the Philippines, especially with the cross-hatching and the slightly mis-proportioned leaf; probably made for the Spanish market or the dance in Indonesia. *Both by courtesy of Martin Willcocks.*

suggests that batik-work is probably of ancient origin. It is a process of dyeing cloth; the area to be left free of dye is coated with a thin layer of wax poured from a small spouted copper vessel. The cloth is dyed, the wax is then removed, and the process is repeated again with more wax and more dye of a different colour until the desired design has been achieved. Older batik fans were created in this way, but modern ones probably have the wax applied with a *tjap*. This is a block or stamp, usually of copper with a raised design. They are often used for border designs in batiks.

Fans could also be made from a textile patterned in *ikat*, where the warp or weft threads are dyed before weaving. It is known in many parts of the world, and in Lombok Island, near Bali, is known as *kain ikat* or *gringsing*, meaning 'flaming cloth'. This is a most intricate and delicate work of art. A far simpler technique is that of block printing on tapa-cloth, made from the bark of the paper-mulberry tree.

LEATHER FANS

Leather fans are used the length and breadth of the archipelago of Indonesia, especially for the dance. There is a costume on view of a Princess of the Court of Surakarta, incorporating a headdress, bodice, *slendang* (sash) and sarong in a pattern exclusive to the Royal Family. When dancing the lady would have used a fan of buffalo hide (fig. 52) decorated with paint and gilded, sometimes with a 'shadow-play' figure on it.

WOODEN FANS

Wooden fans are common to Malaysia. Until recently most Malaysian buildings were made from the wood of the chengal (*Balanocarpus Heimii*), from the Bandi Forest near Kemaman. The Malaysians also made wooden fans, not only for themselves, but also for their flourishing trade of exporting wooden sticks and guards to the fan-makers in Europe in the nineteenth century. The carved decorations all had poetic names, such as 'protracted clouds' (*Awan Larat*), 'young bamboo-shoot design', 'the thundery-weather flower', and so on. Timbers for buildings were usually carved in a recurring motif, yet designs were also

56 Paper advertising fan for a shop in Celebes, now Sulawesi.
Twentieth century.
By courtesy of Martin Willcocks.

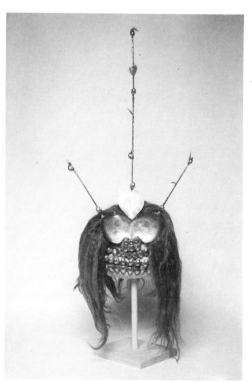

57 Chief's composite headdress from Samoa,
made from yellow hair, shells and three wires
covered and decorated with shells and red feathers.
*By courtesy of the Trustees of the British Museum,
Ethnography Department.*

58 Fan made from akkar-wangi (aromatic roots) ; the mid-rib of a
palm-leaflet holds it in the centre and it has a plaited pandanus
edging. Twentieth century, from the Solomon Islands.
By courtesy of Mrs J. Morris.

59 Folding fan of silk painted in tempera colours, gold and silver. Probably the work of a Court Painter attached to the Royal Palace at Mandalay (Burma) where the fan is stated to be found in 1885.

The subject depicts King Thibaw Min, last King of Burma, with his principal consort Supaya Lat. Circa 1880.
By courtesy of the Victoria and Albert Museum.

60 Composite model of a State Boat from Thailand, nineteenth century. It is made of papier mâché painted red and decorated with elaborate gilded openwork designs, showing many figures holding oars and umbrellas. This State Boat from Bangkok was used in the Kathin River ceremonies, when the King visited the River Temple with gifts.
By courtesy of the Trustees of the British Museum, Ethnography Department.

61 Wooden openwork fan from Tonga, nineteenth century.
*By courtesy of the Trustees of the British Museum,
Ethnography Department.*

62 Composite head-ornament from Telefomin, New Guinea,
nineteenth century. There are eleven cassowary quills set in a lump
of beeswax covered with cloth, each passing through a number of
reed seeds (from the Fal tree) and terminating in a lump of beeswax
set with a white cockatoo feather. Worn by men, sometimes by
women, at singsings, at the back of the head, the cord coming
forward around the forehead.
*By courtesy of the Trustees of the British Museum,
Ethnography Department.*

63 Vegetable fibre plaited fan.
*By courtesy of the Trustees of the British Museum,
Ethnography Department.*

adapted to the general shape of an artifact such as a fan guard or *kris*; woodworkers and metalworkers interchanged their ideas and designs. Many fans were made from sandalwood with chengal guards. Sandalwood is a finely-grained scented wood that has been used from India to China from at least the fifth century BC. The scent comes from the wood's fragrant oil, but insects dislike the smell and will not eat the wood, so a large number of sandalwood fans still survive. The wood was used in Buddhist ceremonies and a magnificent example of a large processional fan for a Buddhist temple is illustrated (fig. 51). There are twenty-five sticks, pierced and serrated, with guards showing typical Malaysian low-relief carving; a pair of carved birds form the handle.

PAPIER MÂCHÉ, GESSO WARES, AND LAC

Most papier mâché work comes from Kashmir. Gesso (varnished) ware comes from Srinagar in Kashmir, Bikaner, and Tonk in northern India, Hyderabad and the Karnul district in the south.

Coarse native paper is softened and mixed with gum, then moulded into the required shape (sometimes with a metal or split-bamboo lining). A coating of white paint is applied, on whose dried surface the colours are drawn with a fine brush. When the painting and gilding are complete, the surface is covered with varnish made from boiling the clearest copal (*sundras*) in pure turpentine. Sometimes mastic varnish (*mustagi rumi*) brought from Kabul was used. There are many fixed fans made from papier mâché and a lobe-shaped example is illustrated (plate 22) which incorporates mica-work.

LAC-WORK

Lac-work, although also made with resin, is quite distinct from Japanese or Chinese lacquer. It is not applied with a brush, but in a solid or half-melted form. In India it is applied mainly to turned woodwork, the sticks of coloured lac being held against the revolving wood and adhering to it with the heat of friction. In Jaipur State, Hoshiapur in the Punjab, and the Maldive Islands, several layers of different colours are laid on and then incised to corresponding depths to show a pattern in various colours. The 'fingernail' technique of Sri Lanka is another method of using lac. A good many fan sticks from India and Sri Lanka show lac-work.

MICA

This is the name given to a group of minerals which include muscovite (potash mica) and phlogopite (magnesia mica). It is found in igneous rocks and splits in one direction only. It can therefore be foliated into very thin sheets which are tough and elastic, do not break easily, but can be scratched with the fingernail.

It is mined in large blocks and then split to the desired size with sharp knives; it is occasionally cut into various shapes, and applied to fans, or even used as peep-holes. It is sometimes also painted. Mica fans today fetch high prices.

VEGETABLE FIBRES

Fans have been made from reeds, *dib*, dry flags, *Typha Augustifolia*, bagar grass, *Eriophorum Cannabinum*, the inner bark of the dhaman (*Grewia Oppositfolia*), *Fothergilla Involucrata*, nettle-bark tree (*Celtis*), *Crotolaria*, *Saccharum Munja*, and a huge variety of palms.

The use of these fibres, barks, and palms is universal in the area covered by this chapter, so it is impossible to say that there is any special locality celebrated for fibrous manufacture. The only time one can safely do so is when a gift is handed in to establishments such as the Museum of Mankind in London (the Ethnography Department of the British Museum) with an accurate provenance.

Some of these materials are plaited, some woven, and some treated in the style of Indian *chicks*, a form of meshed bamboo for screening windows and verandahs. One fan recently bought, and looking like a green *chick* from India, was actually acquired in the depths of Indonesia, highlighting the fact that although there is such a variety of crafts in the East, many of them are practised in every country.

Katy Talati, with her painting materials, seal and seal-ink.
She is showing the position of the hand necessary for
Chinese traditional painting.

Chapter 5 Katy Talati

The paintings of Katy Talati have a special interest in the way they illustrate the very close relationship of pupil and teacher, Katy Talati and Prince P'u Ch'uan, the foremost classical landscape painter of his generation. They illustrate the ability of a sensitive artist to adopt and work in a 'foreign' medium. This aspect of Chinese culture had become a pervading influence in Katy Talati's artistic life and indeed she came to occupy a unique position in the artistic life of Peking where her insight was recognized. She was given a one-man exhibition at the Ashmolean Museum, Oxford, in 1972. This section concentrates on painting techniques, her working materials, and personal artistic memorabilia.

My family have lived in China since the beginning of this century. We were of Persian origin, but came to China from India. The family fortunes were founded by my uncle, who traded between Russia and China. My father was a gentle, artistic man and my mother was musical; my interest in craftsmanship was stimulated by one of the family enterprises, which made both traditional Chinese furniture and hand-made copies of European styles. But my real interest was in painting.

I was given private lessons in Western art at a convent. We were taught to copy Old Masters in oils and watercolours and I dearly wished to travel to Europe to study the originals; but unhappily the 1939 War had started and travel was impractical and difficult.

I turned to the study of the Chinese paintings that were all around me. Once I took this up I realized that for me there was nothing else.

My first master was Father Edmund van Genechten, a Belgian priest, sent by the Pope to Peking for the purpose of painting Christian subjects and scenes in the Chinese style. He taught me mainly landscape painting, but I realized after a while that it was folly to be in China studying Chinese painting under a European.

I also had two other teachers, Wang Huei Hsu, a famous Chinese artist who specialized in figure painting, and Hung Yi, a well-known painter of flowers and birds.

Most of all I loved landscape painting and had, of course, heard of Prince P'u Ch'uan, and it became my ambition to be accepted as one of his pupils. Some pictures of mine were eventually submitted to him (as he was extremely selective) and, to my great joy, I was taken into his studio.

Prince P'u Ch'uan, styled Sung Ch'uan, was a master in the traditional style. He was a member of the last Royal Family in China, a great-grandson of the Emperor Tao Kuang (1821–1851) and the son of Bei Leh Tai Ying. He was born in 1912 and ranked sixth in the Imperial Family.

When the Republic was proclaimed in 1911 Imperial titles were abolished for all except his family, and my teacher was given the title Ch'en-Kuo Chiang-Chun, which means General of the Ch'en-Kuo. Prince P'u Ch'uan's father, an accomplished artist and scholar, undertook the teaching of the Chinese classics to his children. His elder brother, P'u Ch'in (styled Hsüeh-chai) and his cousin P'u Ju (styled Hsin-Yü) were also painters of great distinction. Ever since he was a child he was obsessed with the urge to paint horses. He told me he used to cover the walls of his room (even his pillow-cases and bed-linen) with sketches. I would rate him as one of China's foremost horse-painters. And, naturally, when I painted them I was very much under the influence of his style.

Before I left China towards the end of 1948 Prince P'u Ch'uan was creating a masterpiece. It was a gigantic horizontal scroll which slowly unwound to show horses in different attitudes. His aim was to paint no less than ten thousand horses, and I was fortunate enough to see the scroll when he was almost half-way through. It was a magnificent and ambitious achievement.

He was one of the foremost landscape painters of the time in the north of China. He also painted other subjects such as figures, flowers and birds; these, though, as far as I know, were never to be displayed publicly, they were just personal gifts with special dedications. I am indeed privileged to have several of these, including my 'Farewell Fan' (plate 29).

The inscription shows that he painted it for me on the eve of my departure from China and when translated reads, 'Shun-ming is an expert on Chinese painting. We have so often spent long hours together discussing at great depth the six cannons or principles of Chinese painting. Tomorrow you are leaving for London, so I paint this fan to present to you'.

The six cannons or principles were formulated in the fifth century by Hsieh Ho. Translations differ widely but basically they are:

1 Spirit – or rhythmic vitality
2 Bone structure – or the mastery of the brush
3 Conformity with nature
4 Use of colour to conform with nature
5 Artistic composition
6 The finish – or the transmission of classical models.

These are the principles on which all traditional painting are based.

Shun-ming is my second name, as I have two Chinese names, apart from my surname Ta, which is a transliteration of the sound of the first syllable of my surname Talati. As a small child Chinese friends had given me the popular girl's name of Ai-lien, meaning Beautiful Lotus, and one of my early autograph seals has this name.

When I became a serious artist it was thought that I should have a more scholarly name. So Shun-ming was chosen by my friend Wu Kuang-Yu, the famous figure painter. It is the custom in China that the first character of the name of the eldest child in a family should be used as the first character for all the younger members. My eldest sister, Shireen, was

65 Gold Fan
by Prince P'u Ch'uan

67 'Study of Bambc
by Hsu Shih Hsü

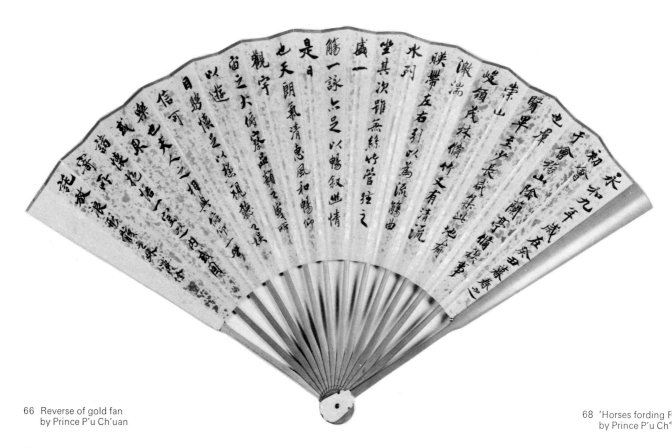

66 Reverse of gold fan
by Prince P'u Ch'uan

68 'Horses fording F
by Prince P'u Ch'

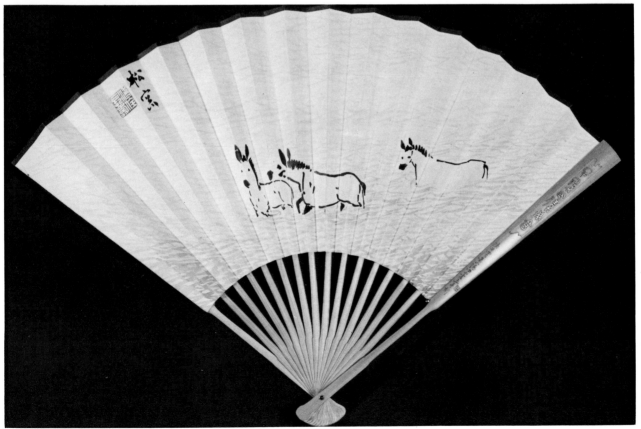

called in Chinese 'Shun Ying' as this was the nearest sound to her own name in Chinese.

The choice of characters is very important, and Shun was chosen after the legendary Emperor Shun whose story is depicted on my 'Named Fan' (plate 28). It illustrates the story (known as *Yao and Shun*) of how the old Emperor Yao travelled throughout his realm in search of a worthy successor. His search ended in a remote village where he came across a humble farmer's lad called 'Shun' who had all the qualities Yao considered essential in his own successor.

In the picture Emperor Yao, with his banner-fan bearer, is offering Shun the reins of the kingdom. Modestly Shun declines. But he does later succeed Yao at his request, and becomes an even greater ruler.

The second half of my name, Ming, is the same character as that of the Ming Dynasty, and means 'brilliant', or 'famous', or 'celebrated'. The three famous Wu brothers painted my 'Named Fan'. The calligraphy on the reverse was done by the eldest, Wu Lü-han, the middle brother Wu Ching-ting was responsible for the landscape, and the youngest brother Wu Kuang-yü painted the figures. Naturally this unique fan is very precious to me.

The War prevented me from continuing my studies throughout the period from the attack on Pearl Harbour in December 1941 till the end of the War in 1945. Peking was under Japanese occupation from 1937 but, as British citizens, our family were not directly affected until the declaration of War between Britain and Japan at the end of 1941. After that we were deprived of our liberty and our property and spent the next three years incarcerated in Weihsien concentration camp in Shantung Province, a virtual no-man's-land. We left our homes with the barest essentials and only as much as each of us could carry. Mercifully, one tends to remember the pleasant side of life, even in a prison camp. One incident gave me back my faith in human nature. On one rare occasion I found time to paint out of doors. Suddenly a shadow fell across my tattered paper. I looked up in fright to see an armed guard behind me. Naturally I expected to be punished but instead the guard smiled and appeared impressed that I, a Westerner, should be practising Chinese painting and calligraphy under those circumstances. The Japanese have a great reverence for Chinese painting. To my great delight this guard, at risk to himself, surreptitiously smuggled a brush and some paper to me the next day.

We returned to a stripped and gutted home, but there was very little left of our wealth apart from the land. After a period of depression and an abortive attempt to reach Europe I returned to life as a painter and scholar and during the next three years I worked with Prince P'u Ch'uan on a treatise on the technique of Chinese Landscape Painting which was completed except for polishing and editing. When I left for England because of the worrying political climate in the east I brought it with me.

When I knew I was to leave China, almost certainly never to return, I decided to bring away some of the work of the most eminent artists and calligraphers in Northern China. I was fortunate enough to find, in an antique shop, a beautiful old album, full of blank silk leaves, which was perfect for this purpose. With the help of Prince P'u Ch'uan and Wu Kuang yü I was able to approach most of the major artists and calligraphers to paint and write in my album – men such as Ch'i Pai-shih (now considered an Old Master) P'u Chin, Ch'en Pan-ting, Ch'i Yuan-po, Hsu Yuan-sun, Wang Hsüeh-tao, Ma Chin and others. It was the greatest honour for me that they agreed to do it. In addition to that, because of the uncertain future, artists endeavoured to surpass themselves as the work was known to be leaving China – for all they knew this album might be their only memorial. It is a unique record and historically significant as possibly the only collective record of the finest Peking artists of the period.

In the early days under Father van Genechten I painted everything on silk. Later I painted mainly on paper. Silk was a popular medium and always has been, although never cheap. It was also available in various different textures. All the leaves in my antique album of contemporary painters and calligraphers are painted on antique silk. For instance my painting 'The Dancers' is on contemporary Chinese silk of a fine grain. The material came in a smooth roll and was cut to the required size. Then I rubbed it all over with talcum powder in case there was any grease. The powder was blown off and then I placed the silk flat on the studio table, laying long heavy weights at each end to hold it in position. It must be remembered that you always work on the flat in China, rather than on a tilted board or standing at an easel like most Western artists. I should add that there are two distinct types of silk, made with either round or flat threads. Before Ch'ien Lung round-threaded silk was used; contemporary silk is flat-threaded. It is still possible to get the round-threaded silk from Japan; it is excellent material because it accepts the ink well.

It is important to remember that all artist's paper was hand-made. The older paper is more mellow and a source of inspiration to the artist. There are two main types of paper in general, either sized or unsized. The unsized is very absorbent and it is essential to work on this extremely rapidly; mistakes can never be erased. There is also a type with flecks of gold or silver which may occasionally be seen in Chinese paper fans. For example, in 'Lady with the Fan under the Wu-tung Tree' there are minute dots of shimmering silver worked into the paper. The piece of calligraphy (on the reverse of Prince P'u Ch'uan's gold fan) (fig. 66) is written with a brush on antique gold-flecked paper. When painting a folding fan the paper was bought pleated and ready-made, in whatever type required, from the artist's shop. In addition to that the fan paper was double, with vertical gaps between for the sticks to be inserted after decoration was complete. A fixed fan was generally made from silk or other materials, but if paper was used it would be doubled – either for strength or for the calligraphy on the reverse.

Prince P'u Ch'uan's framed fan-leaf is on paper covered with pure gold leaf (fig. 76).

The Chinese always made their painting utensils as works of art in their own right, to give them the respect they deserved. To be surrounded by beautiful objects was a source of inspiration to the artist. The brushes differ from European ones in that each is made from several types of hair; the central heart or 'feng' has the strongest hairs and forms the

69 'Boats in a Storm on a Lake'
   by Katy Talati

70 'Willow and Boat'
   by Katy Talati

71 Horse painting, group of eight horses and four grooms
by Prince P'u Ch'uan

72 'Horse and Groom in a Landscape'
by Katy Talati

73 Horse painting, group of eight horses and four grooms with
colophon
by Prince P'u Ch'uan,

74 'Horseman riding through a Cave to the Temple'
by Katy Talati

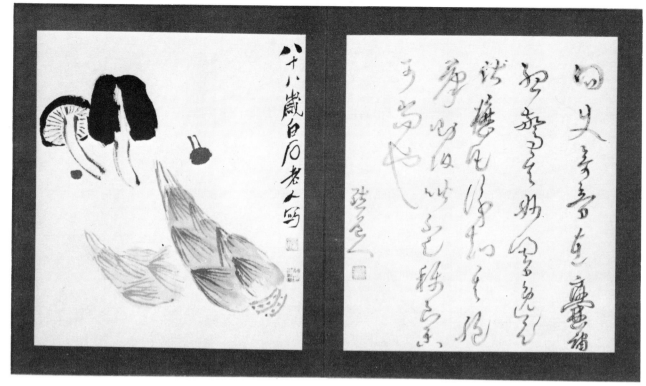

75 Album paintings.
  Ch'i Pai-Shih (still-life) and Prince P'u T'ung (calligraphy), 1948

point. My brushes include the 'Lu-lang hao', a literal translation would be 'deer wolf brush', but in fact it is made from the hairs of the wildcat and weasel or skunk. It is very versatile and favoured by landscape painters because of its flexibility and spring. It is also used for architectural paintings. Goat and rabbit hair brushes are used for colour-washes; another type has a centre of pig bristles and an outer covering of weasel fur – the fur taken from the tail of a weasel in late winter is best and strongest.

The ink is made mainly from lamp-black, pine soot and other ingredients mixed with glue and moulded into cakes or inksticks, often decorated with characters or pictures. Fresh ink is prepared by rubbing the inkstick on an inkstone with a little water and has a great variety of tones ranging from the deepest black to the most pearl grey. This richness and subtlety is perhaps one of the reasons why the Chinese have always liked it. Ink paintings in monotones were much favoured by landscape artists because they created a mood; for example: 'Bamboo Grove by Moonlight' and 'Solitary Boatman' (fig. 78). An inkstone is a slab of blackish-coloured stone of fine quality. You put a little water on your inkstone, then take the inkstick and rub it for a long time on the inkstone, in the water, until it is thick and black. The inkstone is not absorbent, so it prevents the freshly-ground ink from drying quickly. Then you dip your moistened brush into the freshly-made ink and take as much of it as you need for your composition. The same ink is used, undiluted, for all the calligraphy seen on the fans.

I use water colours, never oils, when painting in the Chinese manner. They were sold in tiny packets, some solid and some in powder form. Colours come in two main groups,

vegetable and mineral. Vegetable colours are translucent and indelible (making no allowance for errors). They are mixed with warm water on porcelain palettes and are used in much the same way as water colours in the West. Indigo, rattan yellow and umber are the basic colours, green being made by mixing indigo with rattan yellow. Other colours often used include carmine, 'foreign red', French red and rouge.

Mineral colours are opaque and give a gouache-like effect; they are ground in a pestle and mortar with boiling water and a little freshly-prepared glue. Blues are from lapis lazuli, greens from malachite and vermilion from cinnabar; added to that there is gold leaf and lead white. All these colours are expensive, especially the minerals. Cinnabar, which is also used to make the seal-ink (always red in colour) was weighed on a scale against gold.

Gold comes in either leaf form or as 'wan chin'. This literally translates as 'gold in a bowl'. One buys a tiny porcelain bowl, like a tea-bowl, which is thinly lined with gold of the best quality. To apply it you use a very fine brush dipped into a weak solution of glue, then lift a little gold off the rim of the container, transferring it to the painting.

In China's Golden Age, the T'ang Dynasty, when China was at her greatest both historically and geographically, a group of artists painted mainly in gouache, using blues and greens outlined in gold. Artists at that time came mostly from the aristocracy and, in keeping with royal tastes, they believed in lavishing wealth upon wealth, using expensive mineral colours and gold to enrich their magnificent palaces.

The quality of a Chinese painting is mainly judged by its brushwork and subtlety of ink-tone but composition has particular importance. There is great stress laid on the void

76 Horse painting on gold leaf
by Prince P'u Ch'uan

or blank space left in a picture. An accomplished artist seldom used a preliminary drawing; he would spend most of his time composing his painting in his mind. He would then rapidly transpose his mental image to paper with an economy of strokes. Prince P'u Ch'uan's fan painting 'Horses Fording a River' is a good example, as is Chi Pai-shih's 'Corncobs and Mushrooms' in my album of famous Peking artists. My favourite form of composition is Chinese landscape painting. To me it is synonymous with European music; both forms of art can transport me to sublime heights and it has been described as 'the music of space'. It is little wonder that the Chinese regard landscape painting as the highest form of pictorial art.

The uninitiated Westerner often finds it difficult to appreciate Chinese landscapes, possibly because Western painters have striven to portray the outward appearance of nature, whereas the Chinese aim more to interpret the inner meaning of things. In general the European is accustomed to view a picture with the eye fixed on a single focal point so that the horizon line is placed near the middle of the picture and is painted from the artist's eye-level. Chinese perspective is seen from a height and the line of the horizon is placed very high in a picture. What the Westerner would put in the far distance the Chinese artist will place at the top. A Chinese landscape painting does not have one focal point, it has many. This is known as the principle of the moving focus. That is to say the eye can wander through a landscape and the spectator has the feeling of travelling great distances. There are three main categories of perspective in landscape painting: *the high distance*, where the view is from the foot of a mountain looking up towards the peaks; *the profound or deep*

distance, where the composition is arranged in such a way as to give great depths and distance; and *the level distance*, a view painted from a height looking down. If only the uninitiated could disregard conventional western conventions and could look at a Chinese painting with fresh eyes he stands to gain immense pleasure.

The type of landscape I like best is the mood painting in ink monotones, but that does not mean that I find landscapes in colour inferior. It depends on the individual work; some landscapes have only a suggestion of colour, and there are many techniques of applying it. One method can be illustrated in three stages:

1 The basic composition is sketched out in ink and forms the skeleton or bone structure
2 Tints of umber are then applied to the base of rocks, mountains, and the trunks of trees
3 finally there is an application of translucent washes of either indigo or grass green over the top of rocks, hills, and foliage.

There is an illustration (plate 27) in colour showing the final stage of this process. It is painted on antique paper and is one of the many illustrations in the chapter on the application of colour in the Treatise mentioned before. I have painted several subjects from Chinese mythology, one in particular 'Lady Chang O with Rabbit in the Moon' illustrates the legend of the Lady Chang O, Empress to the wicked Emperor Hou-yi. He had found the elixir of eternal life and was going to drink it. Chang O felt that her husband's immortality would mean eternal misery for the people of China, so she stole the elixir and drank it herself. She became immortal and went to live in the moon, together

77 'Jay on a Branch'
   by Katy Talati

78 'Solitary Boatman'
   by Katy Talati

with the little white rabbit, whom the Chinese traditionally believe lives there.

On a painting there is a signature seal and sometimes extra calligraphy known as the colophon. In other words artists often brought out the essence of their paintings by adding an inscription composed of a piece of poetry or prose; in some cases it may only give the name of the painting and the place and date of origin. If the painting or fan were presented or dedicated then the name of that person also appears. The placing of the colophon helps to balance the composition. It need not be written by the same artist who painted the picture, but as calligraphy and painting are such closely related arts it provides the link between the two. A good example is 'Bamboo and Rocks' by Hsu Shih hsüeh. Here is a rough translation of the colophon: 'With the smoke of the burning incense one can aspire to the teachings of Buddha and can discard the burdens of the business world. One can find peace in the sound of the running stream, the shade of the bamboo grove, the strength and coolness of the rocks, mists and clouds.' If there is a colophon then normally the seal would be placed immediately under the calligraphy, following the artist's signature. If a fan has no colophon the seal is placed at the artist's discretion. Each artist has many seals of varying sizes and shapes – I have five sets – the choice is an integral part of a painting and a matter of discrimination. Each seal is a miniature work of art, carved by a specialist whose mark it bears. It can be made of many different materials and is dipped into the seal-ink (made from a mixture of cinnabar, pure silk, oil, and other ingredients) and then imprinted with a firm and equal pressure on the painting. A good seal colour will not fade for hundreds of years; both the colophon and the seal should play an important role in establishing the authenticity of a painting. You will notice the different placings of the seals in 'Jay on a Branch', 'Horse and Groom in a Landscape', and Prince P'u Ch'uan's gold fan (figs. 65, 76 and 77).

Bibliography

Chapter 1

Crossman, Carl L., *The China Trade*, Princeton 1972 (Chapter 11, Fans).
Giles, H. A., 'Chinese Fans', *Fraser's Magazine*, London, May 1879. Reprinted in Giles, H. A., *Historic China and Other Sketches*, 1882.
Hay, John, 'Chinese Fan Painting', *Colloquies in Art and Archaeology in Asia, no. 5, Chinese Painting and the Decorative Style*, London 1975.
Masterpieces of Chinese Album Painting in the National Palace Museum, Taipei, Taiwan 1971.

Chapter 2

There are few works in English dealing specifically with the Japanese fan but the following are worth mentioning:
Chiba Reiko, *Painted Fans of Japan: Fifteen Noh-Drama Masterpieces*. Rutland, Vermont and Tokyo, Japan, Charles E. Tuttle Company, 1962. Short text with fifteen reproductions. The book itself is fan-shaped.
Hay, John, 'Chinese Fan Painting', in *Chinese Painting and the Decorative Style*, edited by Margaret Medley, London, Percival David Foundation of Chinese Art, 1975. Contains some useful references to early fan history and gives the names of Sung dynasty writers who mention Japanese fans.
Milne Henderson Catalogue: *An Exhibition of Nanga Fan Painting*. London, Milne Henderson, 1975.
Mizuo Hiroshi, *Edo Painting: Sotatsu and Korin*. New York and Tokyo, Weatherhill/Heibonsha, 1972. Introduces the work of two great decorative artists and illustrates many of their fans.
Salwey, Charlotte M. (née Birch), *Fans of Japan*. London, Kegan Paul, Trench, Trübner & Co. Ltd., 1894. Wildly inaccurate and fanciful, but the only work in English devoted to the subject.
Strange, Edward F., *The Colour-Prints of Hiroshige*. London, Cassell & Co. Ltd., 1925. Contains a chapter dealing with Hiroshige's fan prints, based on the Victoria and Albert Museum's collection.

Chapter 4

Mubin Sheppard, *Taman Indera* (Malay Decorative Arts and Pastimes), 1971.
B. H. Baden Powell, *Handbook of the Manufactures and Arts of the Punjab*, 1872.
Soedarsono, *Dances in Indonesia*, 1968.
Pieter Mijer, *Batiks and how to make them*, 1919.
A. K. Coomaraswamy, *Arts and Crafts of India and Ceylon*, 1913.
G. Wooliscroft Rhead, *The History of the Fan*, 1910.

面扇裱

79 Watercolour on paper, depicting the manufacture of folding fans, from an album of trades and occupations.

Chinese, for the Western market, nineteenth century, *By courtesy of the Trustees of the British Museum.*

Acknowledgements

Chapter 3
Acknowledgements and thanks for contributions are due to:
Helen Alexander, Nancy Armstrong, Nicholas Bird, George Borchard, British Museum – Department of Prints and Drawings, Lisa Clinton, Joe Earle, Madame Falluel, Madeleine and Leslie Ginsburg, Avril Hart, Julia Hutt, India Office Library, Donald King, John Irwin, David Levy, Dr Stillfried, Mr Anthony Vaughan, Dr Angela Völker, Dr Christian Witt-Dörring, as well as all those who have so kindly allowed their fans to be used in the exhibitions at Birmingham or in London.

Chapter 4
I wish to acknowledge the considerable help I have been given by:
The British Museum; especially Dr Brian Durrans at the Museum of Mankind and his colleagues at Orsman Road.
Kew Botanical Gardens; especially Miss Rosemary Angel and Miss Laura Ponsonby for identifying Asiatic fibres, etc.
The Victoria and Albert Museum; especially Miss Veronica Murphy and her colleagues in the Indian Department.
Also the Photographic Studios, especially Miss Sally Chappell and Mrs Moira Walters.
No one could have been more kind than the generous lenders, many of whom spent long hours with me (in particular Mrs Nini Trevenen James) explaining about their fans and other artifacts.

Nancy Armstrong

We acknowledge with thanks the contribution from the Worshipful Company of Fan-makers towards this publication.

Photographs have been kindly supplied by lenders and the following photographers:
Sally Chappell
Ian Thomas
Moira Walters

Illustrated on cover:
Chinese, brisé fan in ivory, pierced and painted in gilt and colours. 18th century. *By courtesy of the Victoria and Albert Museum.*